The Bronfman Haggadah

The Bronfman Haggadah

Edgar M. Bronfman

Illustrations by Jan Aronson

RIZZOLI
NEW YORK

New York · Paris · London · Milan

For my beloved wife, Jan Aronson, whose intelligence, kindness, and grace bless me with a renewed vision of my own life, and a deeper connection to the story of the Jewish people, which I retell with her art in these pages. Through her, I have found the one whom my soul loves. (Song of Solomon 3:4)

This book is dedicated to the youth of the Jewish people. We who have come before you stand at the roots of the tree of life, while you rise above us in its blossoming spring. The story of your ancestors is now in your hands. Tell it proudly.

Introduction

Jan and I consider the
Seder a wonderful event for all ages—a way to connect
as Jews in the warm and nurturing environment of the
home. We also believe it is a great opportunity to teach
young people about Judaism. But like many others, we
could not find a *Haggadah* that fulfilled the second task.
So we found ourselves piecing together parts of existing
Haggadot, seeking to make a satisfying whole from many
parts. But that never really worked. So one day I sat
down at my computer and outlined a new *Haggadah*. The
result of this outline rests in your hands. We have tested
it with young people many times, and the overwhelming

reaction we've received has been "Now I understand what Passover is all about." I hope it will have the same result in your family, and that it will contribute to the Jewish renaissance.

*T*he *Bronfman Haggadah,* like more traditional *Haggadot,* provides the *Seder* leader and other concerned adults with the opportunity to teach the essence of Judaism to young people. Toward that end, it offers detailed explanations of all the elements of the *Seder* meal: matzo, a lamb shank bone, parsley, saltwater, *maror, haroset,* the roasted egg, and *afikomen.* However, we've also departed from the traditional material.

When the rabbis wrote the early *Haggadot,* they suppressed the role of Moses in the Exodus narrative. Perhaps

this is because they viewed Moses as a dangerous hero—one who could easily upset the religious hierarchy. I believe this is misguided. Moses is a tremendous example of how questioning the status quo—literally and figuratively—leads to future liberation. That's why this *Haggadah* expands on his role. As you read this booklet, be like Moses: ask and speak up. Free men and women ask questions—slaves cannot.

Another departure from the more traditional *Haggadot* relates to the four kinds of children. We found those narrow definitions difficult to relate to, much less learn from. Instead, we have focused on the four kinds of Jews we are likely to encounter—wise, rebellious, simple, and indifferent. We also took traditional elements and placed them in a different order, infusing new meaning into the text. For example, Jan and I found it odd that Elijah was invited to the table *after* the meal. Surely it is *before* we share in this joyous feast that we should invite strangers into our tent.

Additionally, we've positioned the Exodus story—and its main characters, including God—as metaphor rather than historical fact. We feel this better complements modern sensibilities and makes it easier to absorb the story's timeless lessons.

Finally, this *Haggadah* does not stop after crossing the Sea of Reeds. We continue our *Maggid* or telling of the Passover story to the point when Moses receives the Ten Commandments at Mt. Sinai. I am aware that the holiday of *Shavuot* celebrates this gift to the Jewish people; nevertheless, I thought it important to include in the actual *Seder*. Many people don't celebrate *Shavuot* and if they do, its profound connection to the Passover story is often missed. Yet without the gift of the law, the liberation from Egypt would have quickly descended into anarchy. If the Passover story survived at all, it would be little more than a footnote in history.

My sincere thanks go to the people who helped bring this book to life—first and foremost to Jan Aronson, my beloved wife and the artist whose pictures grace these pages. A most special thank you to Margaret Wolfson, author, storyteller, dear friend, and collaborator, whose research and gift for storytelling and poetry have informed and inspired this version of the *Haggadah*. I also want to thank Dana Raucher, the talented executive director of The Samuel Bronfman Foundation, and finally Rizzoli Publications.

—Edgar M. Bronfman

I was offered the opportunity of a lifetime: to illustrate my husband Edgar's *Haggadah*. More than 124 pages of paintings would be needed, and no one would be looking over my shoulder telling me what to do. I'd have full rein of artistic interpretation—I could do anything I wanted.

"But, Edgar, I'm not an illustrator."

"Good, I don't want an illustrator. I want you to do it."

So began the journey that lasted from mid-December 2010 to mid-September 2011. For the first time in more than forty years as an artist, I completely stopped the work and methods to which I had become accustomed, to focus entirely on making paintings that relate to the beautiful and meaningful text Edgar had been working on for many years. In so many ways this project is a story of love.

The love and respect I have for Edgar and the way we collaborate in life is reflected in this *Haggadah*. As I read the text over and over, I kept looking for meanings that resonated particularly for me. The idea of being welcoming at our *Seder*, and at our table, is profoundly important to me. I instinctively knew that the opening pages should be full of light and fun to look at. Like the seder itself, we were suggesting that this Haggadah would be a little different.

The opening poetry marking God as a metaphor serves as the base on which all the other text is built. Likewise, my paintings draw from an abundance of sources. The abstract patterns come from ancient Egyptian tiles, mummy cases, and relief sculpture; Greek and Roman vase and decorative painting; African textiles. I was inspired to create riffs on these sources and more. While I kept returning to ancient imagery for inspiration for this ancient story, the freedom I had to use anything my imagination could conjure is the fulcrum upon which any success in my efforts is based.

I thought it would be fun to include a biblical map and thus came several days of research to determine what information should be included in the map. I have seen countless illustrated *Haggadahs* and none have included a visual context to the story of the exodus.

I love the open-endedness of our story and that it is impossible to pinpoint specifics. There are five possible sites for Mount Sinai, and there are at least three possible routes taken by the Hebrews—there were established trade routes, important cities flourishing, and various tribes settled among the land. I know that I am not alone in loving maps, so I hope including this one will entertain readers and open their eyes to a new aspect of the Passover story.

Illustrating the finding of Moses's basket presented a conundrum, as I abhor doing the obvious. So instead of concentrating on the story per se, I responded to the vastness of the Nile.

You are asked to look at the breadth of the river and the landscape and how the small basket relates to that.

From a historical point of view, I thought it would be interesting to show what a typical Egyptian house would have looked like and use that image for illustrating the lamb's blood on the lintel and doorposts.

My efforts throughout the project have been to make our *Haggadah* different from the thousands of illustrated *Haggadahs* available. Sometimes I used whimsy to illustrate ideas like the plague of frogs and the song "Dayenu." Sometimes concepts just spoke to me in abstract ways, like the importance of the number 10. I wanted to make the meeting of Aaron and Moses in the desert—two long-lost brothers meeting to collaborate on a plan of momentous proportions—earthy and simple. I had fun with snakes and biting insects but tried to make other paintings, like the quail, oasis, and grape imagery, more elegant.

My research led me to believe that if the Israelites did make a golden idol at Sinai it would have been a bull—not a calf. Our people spent many years in Egypt, and they would have brought with them the relics of their environment. They would have made a bull idol, as that was what was typical of them. Thus, I illustrated a golden bull in the same style as an Egyptian idol.

The last page of the *Haggadah* speaks of freedom. This is a concept of tremendous importance, and the last thing I wanted to do was to strike up the visual band and scream Edgar's poetry. I encased his last two stanzas in feathers and toned down the color so that the words and images would work together.

I loved working on this project and believe that the intense focus needed to create these paintings changed my life. The ten months of being away from what I'd become accustomed to in the studio created some stress, but I loved doing the research that opened my mind to new ideas and allowed me to learn more about a holiday I had celebrated for so many years.

As an artist I loved the format of my paintings and their intimate size, and what I learned in creating them. But I go back to the ultimate gift of creating these illustrations, and that is collaborating with Edgar. He is profoundly generous and eternally interesting.　　　—Jan Aronson

WELCOME

LEADER: I welcome all of you to our Passover—a festival of freedom that the Jewish people have been celebrating for thousands of years. In celebrating this holiday, we fulfill the injunction in the Book of Exodus: "Remember the day you came forth from bondage in Egypt and recount it to the generations."

The jewel in the crown of the weeklong Passover holiday is the *Seder*—a special feast that contains all the elements of basic Judaism. We learn about our people's deliverance from slavery and the importance of loving the stranger. We learn about gratitude and the Jewish way of celebrating spring. Above all, we learn that freedom is inseparable from moral responsibilities.

LEADER: Our guide for tonight's ceremony is a special booklet called the *Haggadah*. The *Haggadah*, which began thousands of years ago as a spare text of some 450 words, evolved over the centuries into a dense and at times bewildering compilation of rituals, blessings, prayers, stories, and commentary. This greatly embellished text is considered the traditional *Haggadah*.

However, in recent years, the traditional text has undergone extensive revision. These newer editions, which number in the thousands, have streamlined the older material and infused it with new meaning. Some, like this version, have gone even further — replacing the notion of a personal, supernatural, and anthropomorphic "God" with one that better complements contemporary sensibilities. In this *Haggadah*, "God" is understood as "energy" — an energy that is both transcendent (beyond us) and immanent (within us).

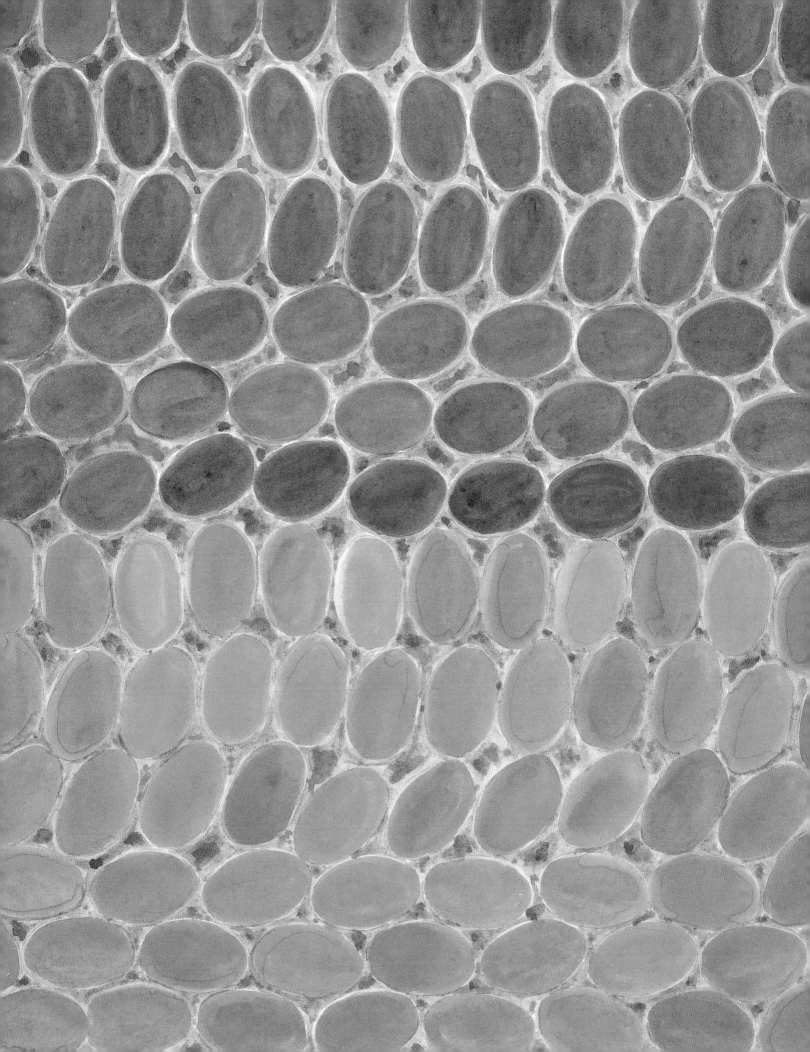

CELEBRANT:

In its transcendent form, this energy lives in comets sparkling through the sky . . .

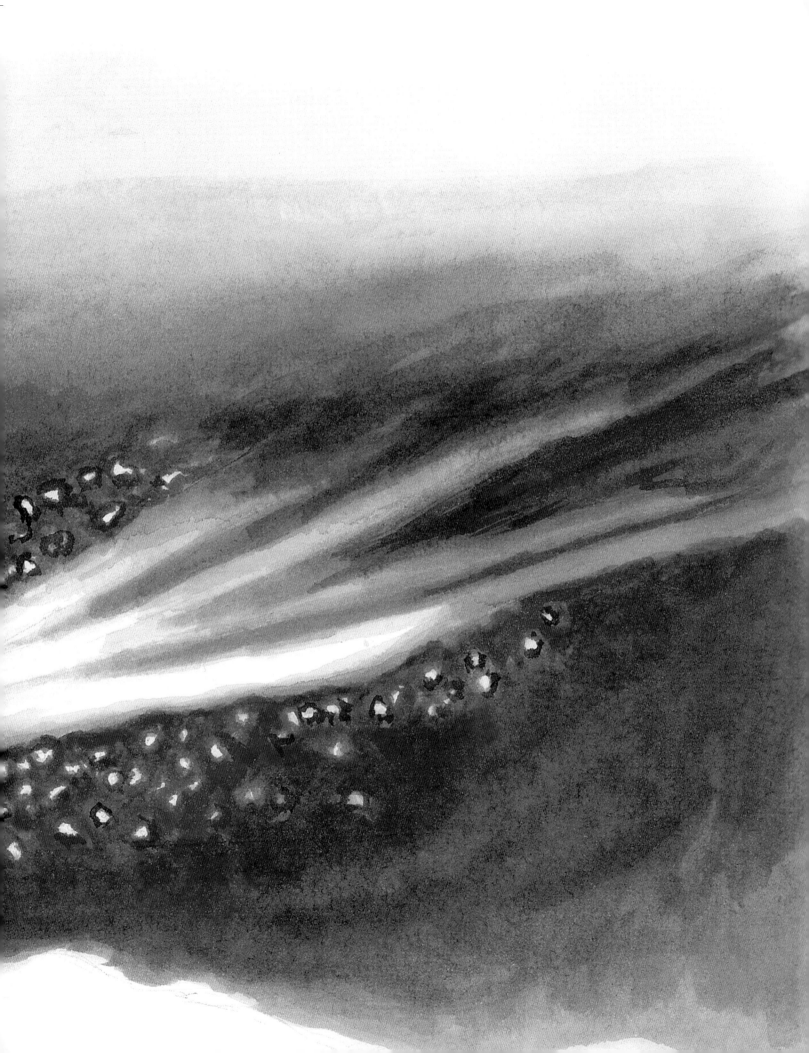

CELEBRANT:

and fish, swimming through the sea.

CELEBRANT:

It is visible in a plum rounding on the bough . . . and the tendrils of a seed, unfurling in the ground.

CELEBRANT:
It is heard in the babble of babies…

CELEBRANT:
and the wise words of elders.

CELEBRANT:

We feel it in the coolness of the night .

nd the heat of the day.

CELEBRANT: I t keeps billions of galaxies from colliding . . .

CELEBRANT: and builds a single grain of sand from a trillion molecules.

CELEBRANT: Yet in the end, even if the skies were made of parchment, all the reeds quills, all the seas and water made of ink, and every person on earth a scribe*, it would be impossible to describe, much less understand, this transcendent energy. All we can safely posit is this: in its transcendent form, this energy does not intervene in our personal, social, or political affairs.

LEADER: However, we can understand this energy in its immanent form. Simply, it is the "godliness" within us. It is expressed when a father plays with his child . . .

CELEBRANT: or nations collaborate on the problem of climate change.

CELEBRANT: It is found in the beauty and power of our artistic works . . .

CELEBRANT: and in our generous and kindly actions—for example, when doctors perform operations for those who lack the means to pay, when parents bless their children at the Sabbath table, and when teachers patiently guide students through their studies.

CELEBRANT: And it is always present when we selflessly stand up for those in peril or want.

*Rabbi Meir Ben Isaac Nehorai

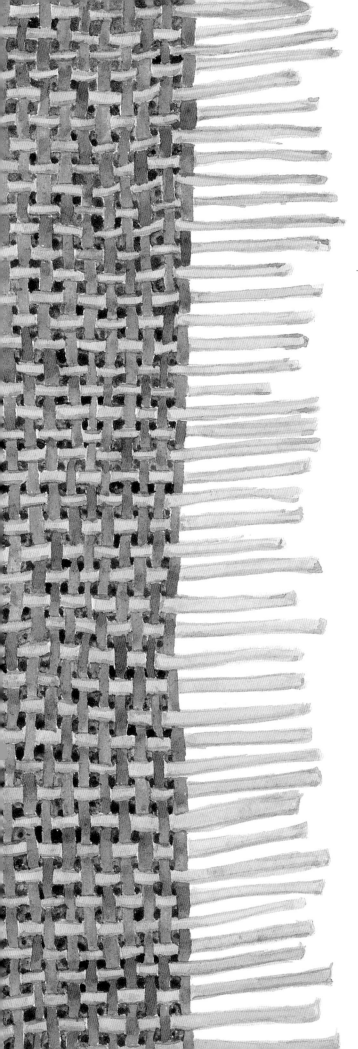

LEADER:

Although we can never know the loom, we do know the weaver — and he is each of us. On the warp and woof of our words and deeds, we create the fabric both of our lives and of our communities. This Passover season, let us dedicate ourselves to weaving a sturdier, more vibrant, more beautiful cloth.

LEADER: As has been the custom for centuries, we traditionally open a door during the *Seder*, inviting the Prophet Elijah to join our celebration. Elijah represents a redeemed world—a world free of racism, slavery, cruelty, poverty, and greed. The wine in his decorated cup symbolizes that joyful world—a world that Jews are commanded to build.

CELEBRANT: Elijah also represents the hungry stranger. And while we don't literally expect strangers to walk through the door, this gesture reminds us to open the doors of our hearts to those in need during this holiday season and in the days beyond. *(Leader asks a child to open the door.)*

Festival Candles and Blessings

LEADER: One of the most intriguing aspects of the *Seder* is how it conveys ideas through physical, verbal, and musical modes. The *Seder* officially begins with a physical action: the lighting of candles. In ancient times, candles—or, most probably, oil lamps—were the only source of light after sunset. Since Jewish holy days always begin after sunset, lights were necessary for any observance. The candles remain an important part of our ceremony—their wavering fire reminds us of the importance of keeping the fragile flame of freedom alive in the world.
(Leader asks that the candles be lit while reciting the blessing.)

We gather together to tell the story of our ancestor's freedom from bondage in Egypt, for it is written: you shall celebrate the Feast of Unleavened Bread and observe this day from generation to generation.

As we light the festival candles, we acknowledge that as match, wick, and wax brighten our Passover table, good thoughts, good words, and good deeds brighten our days.

LEADER: We now say *Kiddush*—a blessing that designates a person, place, thing, or time for a higher purpose.

CELEBRANTS IN UNISON:

There is no beautifier of complexion, or form, or behavior like the wish to scatter joy and not pain around us.

—Ralph Waldo Emerson

LEADER: Along with celebrating our ancestor's deliverance from bitter bondage in Egypt, the Passover holiday highlights the importance of hope. And what better time to celebrate hope than spring? Understanding this, our sages wisely folded the Passover celebration into the ancient Israelite agricultural event *Hag Ha Aviv*—the Holiday of Spring. As life breaks free of winter's icy locks, we are reminded of our capacity for renewal. In homage to this season of rebirth, we read a short passage from the *Song of Songs*, a love song in the Hebrew Bible:

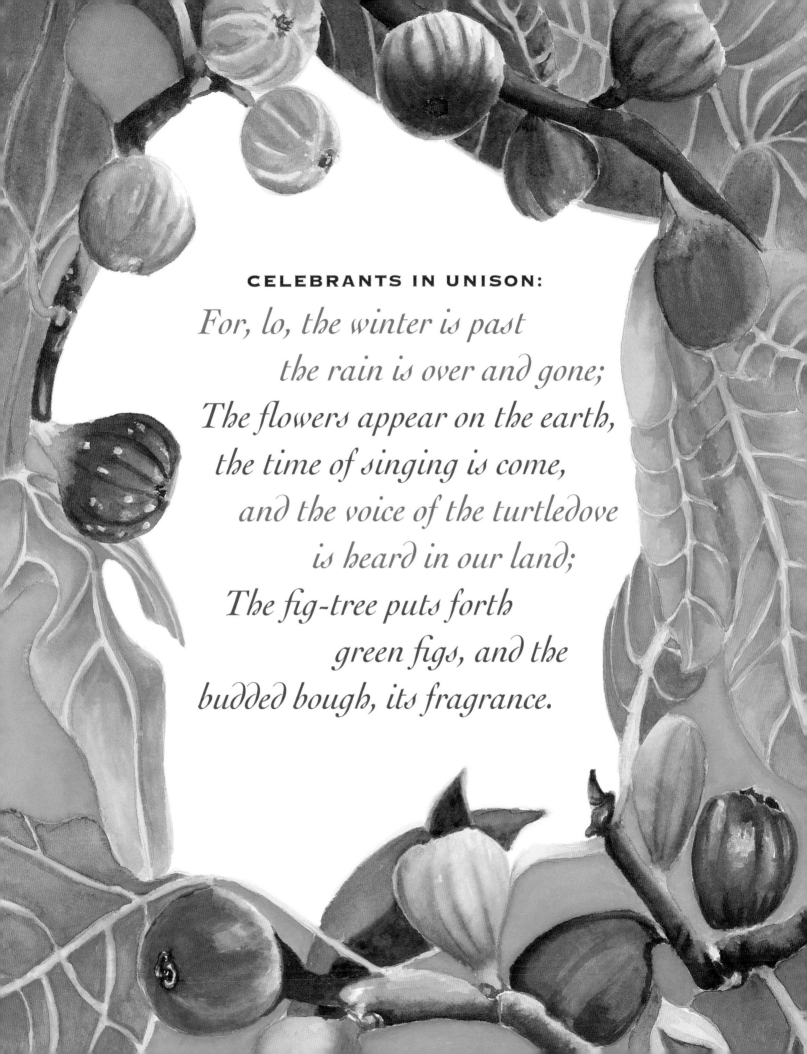

CELEBRANTS IN UNISON:

For, lo, the winter is past
the rain is over and gone;
The flowers appear on the earth,
the time of singing is come,
and the voice of the turtledove
is heard in our land;
The fig-tree puts forth
green figs, and the
budded bough, its fragrance.

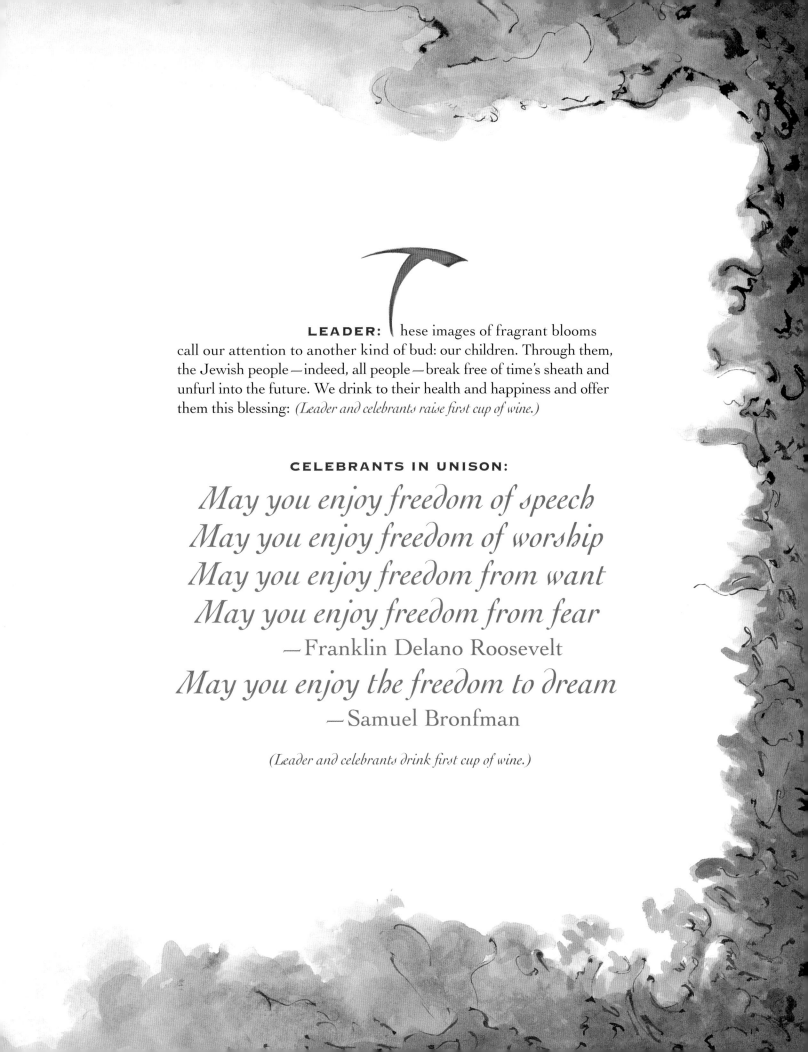

LEADER: These images of fragrant blooms call our attention to another kind of bud: our children. Through them, the Jewish people—indeed, all people—break free of time's sheath and unfurl into the future. We drink to their health and happiness and offer them this blessing: *(Leader and celebrants raise first cup of wine.)*

CELEBRANTS IN UNISON:

May you enjoy freedom of speech
May you enjoy freedom of worship
May you enjoy freedom from want
May you enjoy freedom from fear
—Franklin Delano Roosevelt
May you enjoy the freedom to dream
—Samuel Bronfman

(Leader and celebrants drink first cup of wine.)

Passover's Symbolic Foods

LEADER: To set the stage for our recital of the Exodus narrative, we taste and talk about the ceremonial foods on or near the *Seder* plate. We begin with the *matzah*.
(Leader holds up or points to a single piece of matzah.)

Some call this dry, almost tasteless cracker the bread of affliction—the food of slaves. As such, it memorializes the tasteless fare we ate as slaves in ancient Egypt. Others see it as a delicious food, emblematic of our people's first steps toward freedom. As described in the Book of Exodus, the Israelites departed Egypt in such haste that their bread had no time to rise.

baytzah

matzah

maror

zoroa

karpas

CELEBRANT:

Matzah
Flat you are as a doormat
and as homely.
No crust, no glaze, you lack
a cosmetic glow.
You break with a snap.
You are dry as a twig
split from an oak
in midwinter.
You are bumpy as a mud basin
in a drought.
Square as a slab of pavement,
you have no inside
to hide raisins or seeds.
You are pale as the full moon
pocked with craters.
What we see is what we get,
honest, plain, dry
shining with nostalgia
as if baked with light
instead of heat.
The bread of flight and haste
in the mouth you
promise, home.
— Marge Piercy

LEADER: We now perform a long-standing *Seder* ritual called *yachetz* (*ya-KETZ*)—the breaking of the middle *matzah*. *(Leader holds up matzah and breaks it into two pieces.)*

Over time, this custom accrued multiple meanings. Some believe it represents the parting of the sea; others, the breaking apart of slavery's shackles. It could also remind us of the two great events in our ancestors' quest for freedom: the escape from physical bondage in Egypt and the receiving of the Ten Commandments in Sinai.

CELEBRANT:

But whatever meaning we ascribe to this ritual breaking, one thing is clear — as long as the rights of others are violated, none of us can be truly whole.

Zeroa

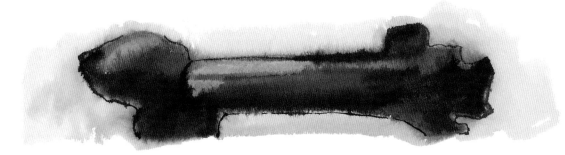

LEADER: We now turn our attention to the *zeroa* (ZE-RO-AH), a roasted lamb shank bone.
(Leader holds up or points to lamb shank bone on Seder plate.)

This item is associated with the holiday's name—*Pesach*—a word meaning to "pass through," to "pass over," to "exempt or spare." To combat Pharaoh's repeated refusal to free the Hebrew slaves, God—whom our ancestors considered the most powerful in the region's pantheon of supernatural gods—sent a tenth plague.

CELEBRANT: According to the Exodus narrative, God informs Moses that the Angel of Death will sweep over Egypt, destroying all the firstborn male children and animals. To protect themselves from this terrible scourge, the Israelites are instructed to daub their doorposts and lintels with the blood of an unblemished lamb. Seeing the marks, the Angel of Death will "pass over" their homes. The lamb shank bone commemorates this event.

CELEBRANT: As with all the ritual foods of the *Seder*, other interpretations abound. Some believe that because the lamb was a sacrificial animal, the shank bone can remind us of the sacrifices made for freedom, something never easily won. In the powerful words of Frederick Douglass, the nineteenth-century Abolitionist:

If there is no struggle, there is no progress.
Those who profess to favor freedom,
and yet deprecate agitation,
are men who want crops
without plowing up the ground,
they want rain without
thunder and lightning.
They want the ocean without
the awful roar of its many waters.

Tonight, we express our gratitude to all the men and women who sacrificed their own lives so we could live in freedom today.

Karpas

(Leader points to or holds up parsley.)

LEADER: Another symbolic food on the *Seder* plate is the *karpas* (*kar-PAS*) — a Greek word meaning "appetizer." In ancient times, appetizers or dipped foods were available only to free citizens. Tonight — as an emancipated people — we enjoy the privilege of dipping our food.

CELEBRANT: However, we don't dip our sprig of parsley into a sweet or tangy sauce. Instead, we dip it in salted water. The salt water symbolizes the sweat and tears our ancestors shed as slaves in Egypt, the tears shed under Crusader persecutions in the Holy Land, and those cried...

CELEBRANT: during expulsion from Spain…

CELEBRANT: pogroms in Russia…

CELEBRANT: and torture and murder at the hands of the Nazis and their sympathizers.

LEADER: In remembrance of our slain forebears—and all the other people, Jews and non-Jews, whose lives have been crushed by tyrants, we take sprigs of parsley and dip them in bowls of salted water. *(Celebrants pass around parsley sprigs and dip into bowl or bowls of salt water.)*

CELEBRANT: But although millions of our people were destroyed, we endure. To symbolize and celebrate the triumph of life over death, we dip our parsley—a spring vegetable—into the salt water. *(Celebrants dip parsley into salt water a second time.)*

CELEBRANT: There is another, more recent meaning associated with the parsley. As a green plant, it reminds us of the ecological laws laid out in the Torah thousands of years ago. These laws—the *bal tashchis*—prohibit wanton destruction or waste of resources. This Passover season, in the spirit of *Tikkun Olam* (repairing the world), we dedicate ourselves—in whatever ways we can—to halting the ruin of our planet—its water, soil, and air.

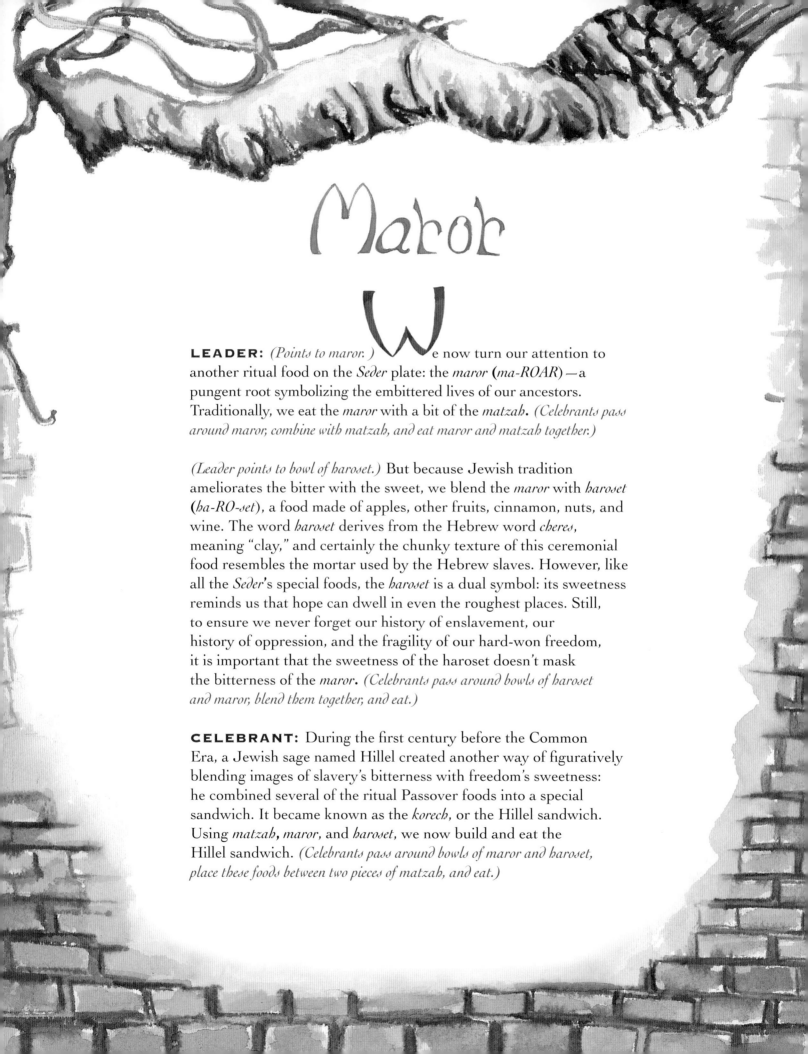

Maror

LEADER: *(Points to maror.)* We now turn our attention to another ritual food on the *Seder* plate: the *maror* (ma-ROAR)—a pungent root symbolizing the embittered lives of our ancestors. Traditionally, we eat the *maror* with a bit of the *matzah*. *(Celebrants pass around maror, combine with matzah, and eat maror and matzah together.)*

(Leader points to bowl of haroset.) But because Jewish tradition ameliorates the bitter with the sweet, we blend the *maror* with *haroset* (*ha-RO-set*), a food made of apples, other fruits, cinnamon, nuts, and wine. The word *haroset* derives from the Hebrew word *cheres*, meaning "clay," and certainly the chunky texture of this ceremonial food resembles the mortar used by the Hebrew slaves. However, like all the *Seder*'s special foods, the *haroset* is a dual symbol: its sweetness reminds us that hope can dwell in even the roughest places. Still, to ensure we never forget our history of enslavement, our history of oppression, and the fragility of our hard-won freedom, it is important that the sweetness of the haroset doesn't mask the bitterness of the *maror*. *(Celebrants pass around bowls of haroset and maror, blend them together, and eat.)*

CELEBRANT: During the first century before the Common Era, a Jewish sage named Hillel created another way of figuratively blending images of slavery's bitterness with freedom's sweetness: he combined several of the ritual Passover foods into a special sandwich. It became known as the *korech*, or the Hillel sandwich. Using *matzah*, *maror*, and *haroset*, we now build and eat the Hillel sandwich. *(Celebrants pass around bowls of maror and haroset, place these foods between two pieces of matzah, and eat.)*

Baytzah

LEADER: The last item on our *Seder* plate is a *baytzah* (*bay-TSAH*), or roasted egg, an item almost universally associated with rebirth and spring. This beautiful symbol reminds us that renewal is always possible—no matter how broken or bitter the past.

We conclude our discussion of the *Seder* plate foods by hiding the bigger half of the broken *matzah*. This half is called the *afikomen* (*ah-fee-KO-man*), a Greek word meaning "dessert" or "revelry." At the end of the Passover meal, the children will look for the *afikomen*, and the child who finds it will receive a prize. The service cannot continue after the meal until the *afikomen* has been found. This custom developed as a way of keeping the children awake so they could receive the evening's true treasure—a deeper understanding of freedom and the moral responsibilities that go with it. (*Leader hides the afikomen.*)

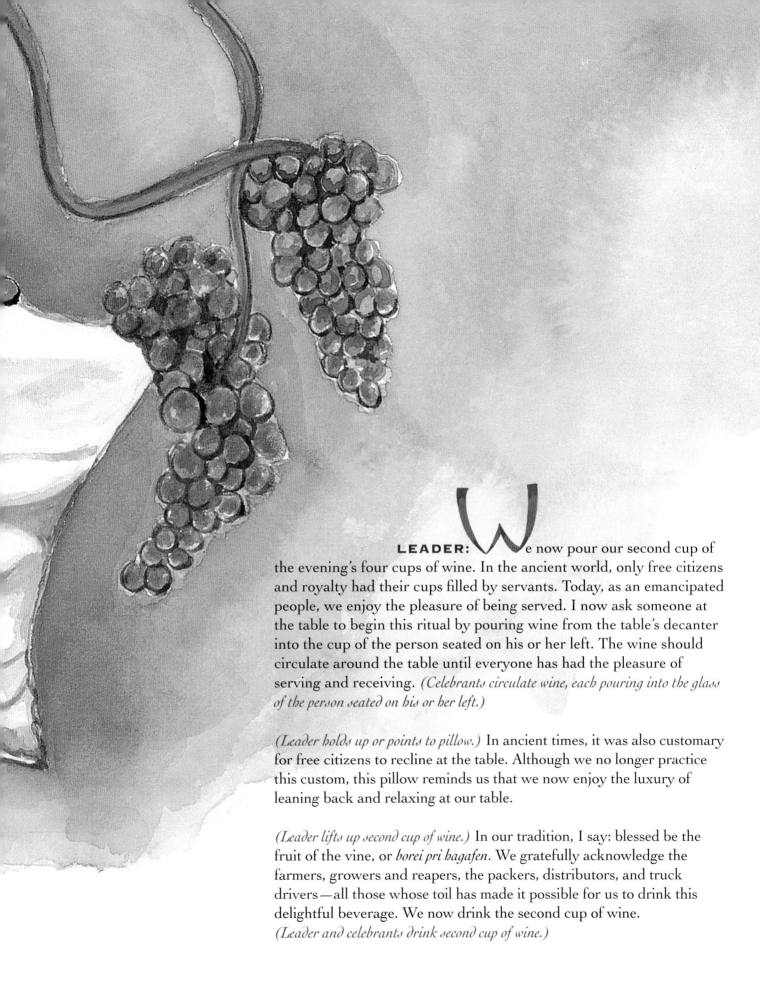

LEADER: We now pour our second cup of the evening's four cups of wine. In the ancient world, only free citizens and royalty had their cups filled by servants. Today, as an emancipated people, we enjoy the pleasure of being served. I now ask someone at the table to begin this ritual by pouring wine from the table's decanter into the cup of the person seated on his or her left. The wine should circulate around the table until everyone has had the pleasure of serving and receiving. *(Celebrants circulate wine, each pouring into the glass of the person seated on his or her left.)*

(Leader holds up or points to pillow.) In ancient times, it was also customary for free citizens to recline at the table. Although we no longer practice this custom, this pillow reminds us that we now enjoy the luxury of leaning back and relaxing at our table.

(Leader lifts up second cup of wine.) In our tradition, I say: blessed be the fruit of the vine, or *borei pri hagafen*. We gratefully acknowledge the farmers, growers and reapers, the packers, distributors, and truck drivers—all those whose toil has made it possible for us to drink this delightful beverage. We now drink the second cup of wine.
(Leader and celebrants drink second cup of wine.)

LEADER: The traditional *Haggadah* speaks of Four Children—one who is wise, one who is wicked, another who is simple, and one who does not know to ask. The Four Children ask questions and receive answers about the Seder in ways appropriate to their intellectual or emotional level. In this *Haggadah*, the children are recast as four types of Jews: the wise, rebellious, simple, and indifferent.

CELEBRANT: The wise Jew ceaselessly challenges conventions; he is fully dedicated to improving Judaism. Despite obstacles, he presses forward, committed to finding better ways to blend Judaism with modern life. These Jews are essential to keeping Judaism a vital force. As such, we must fully support them in their quest, fully embracing their doubts and questions.

CELEBRANT: Unlike the wise Jew, the rebellious Jew has little interest in Judaism because he feels personally or politically excluded. We must embrace these rebellious Jews, address their anger, and when appropriate, champion their causes.

CELEBRANT: The simple Jew is one with a loose connection to Judaism; he neither doubts nor seeks to improve the tradition. Because these Jews can easily slip into indifference, it is critical to find ways of more deeply engaging them in Jewish life.

CELEBRANT: The Jew in greatest danger is the indifferent Jew. Unlike the simple Jew, the indifferent Jew has removed himself entirely from the tradition. While challenging, it is our responsibility to reach out to indifferent Jews, gently inviting them back into the fold.

LEADER: The number four also comes into play in the *Seder's* Four Questions — really one question with four examples. Not only does this ritual reinforce what they've just learned about the *Seder's* ceremonial foods, but the act of questioning reminds us that we have the luxury of fulfilling our intellectual curiosity.

The *Talmud*, a collection of commentaries and laws relating to the Hebrew Bible, urges everyone — young and old, learned and unschooled, male and female — to ask questions. As the Jewish inventor Charles Steinmetz said, "No man really becomes a fool until he stops asking questions."

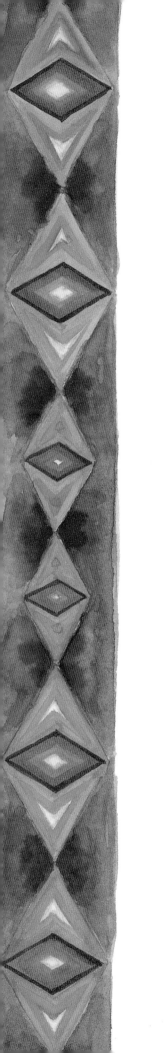

One Question, Four Examples

LEADER: *Ma nishtano ha-lailo ha-zeh meekol ha-laylot* — "Why is this night different from all other nights?" This is the key question, traditionally asked by the youngest speaking child at the *Seder*. To help elicit the child's responses, we pose this overarching question as four shorter ones. In this *Haggadah*, we've added another question, at the start. *(Leader selects a child, or children, to ask questions.)*

CHILD: Why did our sages want the youngest child at the table to ask the questions?

LEADER: If a child is old enough to sit at the table, he or she should be old enough to ask questions. Our Talmud insists on our asking questions, which free people can and must do.

This makes Judaism different from the other monotheistic religions, as we are expected to doubt.

CHILD: Why do we eat *matzah* on this night?

LEADER: Tonight we eat flat bread or *matzah*—not leavened bread, bread that is fluffy—to help us remember how hastily the Hebrew slaves left Egypt.

CHILD: Why do we eat *maror*—bitter herbs—on this night?

LEADER: The bitter taste of the *maror* reminds us of our ancestors' embittered history.

CHILD: Why do we dip our parsley in salted water twice?

LEADER: The salt water represents the tears shed by our ancestors as slaves in Egypt and throughout their painful history. We dip the parsley in a "bowl of tears" to commemorate the suffering that Jews and non-Jews endured under ruthless regimes. The sprig of parsley also serves as a symbol of spring, teaching us never to let go of hope. Finally, as a green plant, it reminds us to take care of our planet Earth—the only home we have ever known.

CHILD: Why do we drink wine and have a pillow at the Passover table?

LEADER: In ancient times, only free citizens could drink wine and recline or relax at the table. Although once we are slaves, we are now free. To celebrate our freedom, we have a pillow at our table and enjoy wine with our family and friends.

LEADER:

And speaking of enjoyment — there is nothing more enjoyable than a good story. With that in mind, we move to the Maggid section of our ceremony — a Hebrew word meaning "to tell."

The Telling

CELEBRANT: Like the *Haggadah*, the Book of Exodus was created over a long span of time by many authors. While the story's historicity hasn't been proven, it isn't pure invention either.

CELEBRANT: Like the rest of the Bible, the Book of Exodus is a mix of history, myth, and legend. And while aspects of the narrative don't reflect today's sensibilities, the story remains an astonishing one—particularly in light of when it was created.

CELEBRANT: Until this narrative, no story took the freeing of slaves as its central theme. No story focused so insistently on the idea that societies must be ruled by moral laws. And while other ethical guidelines preceded the Ten Commandments—notably Hammurabi's Code, the Hebrew Bible's Noahadic Laws, and the precepts of Buddhism—the Exodus narrative is unique, as it asserts that the condition of freedom is inextricably linked to the practice of moral responsibilities.

BIBLICAL MAP OF THE EXODUS

—————— SUSPECTED ROUTE

• • • • • ALTERNATE SUSPECTED ROUTE

—————— CENTRAL ROUTE

– – – – – ALTERNATE CENTRAL ROUTE

—————— NORTHERN ROUTE

—————— MAJOR ROADS

✴ POSSIBLE LOCATIONS FOR MT. SINAI

■ TWELVE TRIBES OF ISRAEL

DAMASCUS

SIDON

TYRE

ASHER

NAPHTALI

DAN

AKKO

ZEBULUN

LAKE CHINERET

GOLAN

DOR

MEGIDDO

ISAAC

EAST MANASSEH

MANASSEH

EPHRAIM

GAD

RABBAH

THE GREAT SEA

JOPPA

BENJAMIN

JERUSALEM

DAN

BEZER

RUEBEN

C A N A A N

JUDAH

SALT SEA

ASHOD

HEBRON

DIBON

GAZA

BEERSHEBA

SIMEON

MIGDOL

EL-ARISH

KADESH

OBOTH

SILE

PUNON

RAAMSES

WILDERNESS OF ZION

PITHOM

JABEL HELAL

EDOM

SUCCOTH

ISMALIA

WILDERNESS OF SHUR

LAND OF GOSHEN

MIGDOL

ON (HELIOPOLIS)

WILDERNESS OF PARAN

PI-HAHIROTH

MARAH

EZION-GEBER

OPH (MEMPHIS)

JEBEL SIN BISHER

RED SEA

ELIM

SINAI

GULF OF AQABA

DOPHKAH

NUWEIBA

M I D I A N

HAZOROTH

EGYPT

ALASH

JEBEL SERBAL

REPHIDIM

DAHAB

EL-KHROB

MT. SINAI

CELEBRANT: Given the unique connection our sages forged between freedom and morality, it is not surprising that the Exodus narrative has served as an inspiration and touchstone for political and social movements seeking societal improvement through the creation of just and ethical laws.

LEADER: Before we recite a simplified version of this fascinating story of deliverance, I encourage everyone to think of it as literature—that is, metaphorically. In this context, for example, the burning bush might stand for the endurance of Judaism, its indestructibility.

CELEBRANT: Pharaoh might represent greed, selfishness, and cruelty—characteristics we must overcome if we are to be free of our own enslavement to destructive impulses that are so entrenched they can easily drown out the voice of reason.

CELEBRANT: Moses could stand for our conscience—the voice of morality and ethics.

CELEBRANT: And God could symbolize the "godliness" within—the force that encourages us to bring ourselves and others out of the cramped mudflats of oppression and into the large and lovely land of freedom.

LEADER: As our sages suggested, the *Seder* should be both solemn and lively. It should also keep the attention of young and mature participants alike. In service of "lively," and to make the *Seder* more accessible to children, this *Haggadah* features the Exodus narrative as Reader's Theater.

NOTE TO LEADER: The reading should be done in a circle, with Seder participants taking turns reading characters' or narrators' parts. Each capitalized heading signals a shift to the next reader.

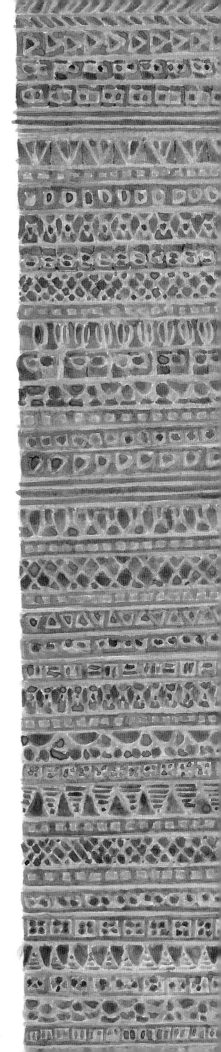

Exodus Script

NARRATOR: Four hundred years before the Exodus, a Hebrew named Joseph lived in the land of Egypt. Originally from Canaan, Joseph had been sold into slavery by his jealous brothers. His extraordinary ability to interpret dreams eventually won his freedom and rose to prominence in Egypt

NARRATOR: When a severe famine ravaged the area, Joseph reconciled with his brothers and brought his extended family from Canaan, settling them in Goshen, one of Egypt's most fertile regions. As Joseph's brilliant rationing strategies spared Egypt the worst of the famine, he was revered by the Egyptians.

NARRATOR: This love extended to his tribe—the Hebrews, or Israelites. But hundreds of years later, a Pharaoh came to power who didn't know of Joseph and his legacy. And this Pharaoh feared the Israelites' numbers.

PHARAOH: Our land teems with Israelites! Should war break out, they could easily side with the enemy. We must keep them from multiplying!

NARRATOR: So Pharaoh assigned two Hebrew midwives—Shiprah and Puah—with the terrible task of killing all the Hebrew boy babies at birth. But the midwives thwarted Pharaoh's order.

NARRATOR: So Pharaoh set taskmasters over the Israelites, hoping to deplete their vigor with hard labor. Still, the Hebrew population swelled. Furious, Pharaoh ordered his soldiers to find every firstborn Hebrew boy and cast him into the Nile.

NARRATOR:

Now there was a Hebrew mother named Jocheved. Often she'd seen Pharaoh's daughter and her maidservants bathe in a pool sheltered by reeds. So Jocheved, with her daughter Miriam, set to work, daubing a bulrush basket with pitch and clay. With the watertight basket, they set off for the pool. Once there, they placed the little ark among the reeds.

NARRATOR: Unable to watch her child be claimed by another, Jocheved returned to Goshen. But Miriam stayed behind, wanting to know her baby brother's fate. Soon Pharaoh's daughter came to the river. When she spotted the basket, she commanded a servant to draw it from the water. Looking down at the little face, her heart filled with compassion for what she quickly realized was a Hebrew infant, most likely hidden by a desperate mother. She turned to one of her servants.

PRINCESS: My baby needs a wet nurse. Find one!

NARRATOR: Miriam stepped out from hiding.

MIRIAM: I know a woman who can nurse your baby.

PRINCESS: Well, go then and fetch her!

NARRATOR: Miriam hastened to Jocheved and told her what happened. And Jocheved suckled the baby, whom the princess named Moses—a common Egyptian name, but one that in Hebrew means "drawn from the water."

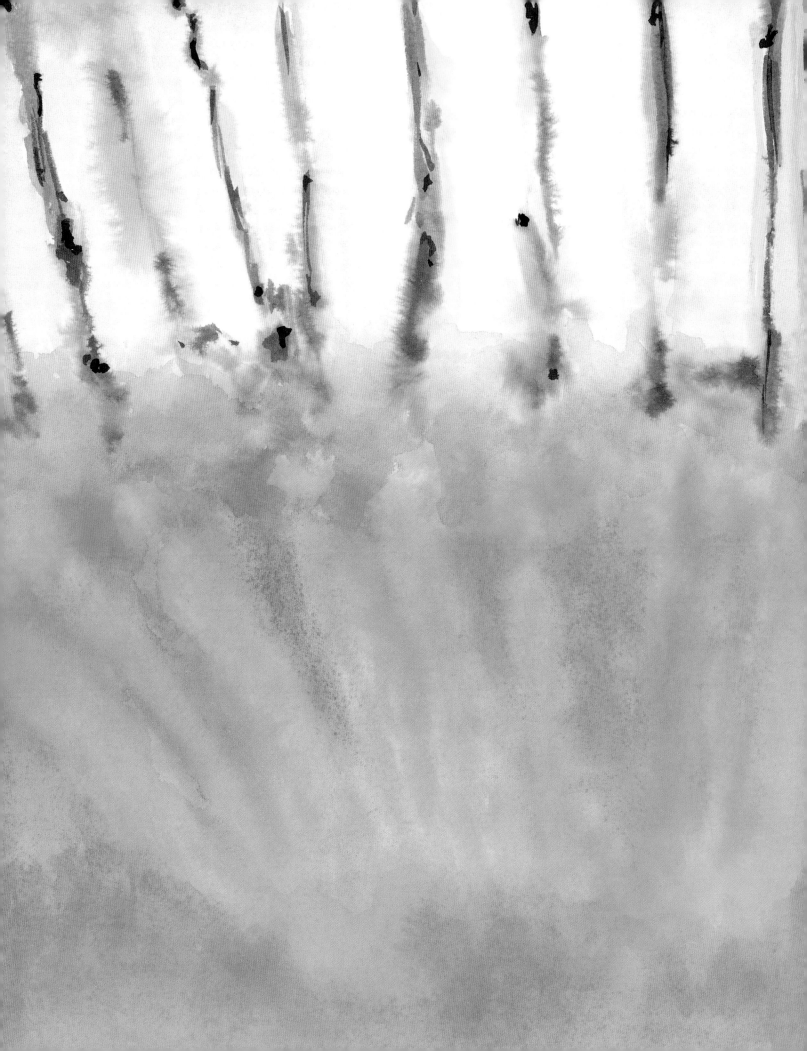

NARRATOR: Moses grew up with Pharaoh's son. They played together, rode horses together, and were like brothers. But Moses often felt a strange longing—especially when he watched the Hebrews toiling under the scorching sun, forced to build the treasure cities of Ramses and Pithom. The feeling deepened until one day when, as a whip whistled over the back of an elderly Hebrew, it erupted.

MOSES: Stop! You must stop!

NARRATOR: When the slave driver ignored Moses' command, Moses killed him and hid the body in the sand. But one of Pharaoh's men witnessed the killing. When he learned of it, Pharaoh shouted:

PHARAOH: Find Moses! He must be punished!

NARRATOR: *B*ut Moses had already escaped. He was now sojourning in the desert, seeking a home far from the tyranny and temples of Egypt. When he reached a place called Midian, he married a young woman named Zipporah—daughter of Jethro, a priest and shepherd. And Zipporah bore him two sons, and Moses dwelt with his family in Midian for many years.

NARRATOR: One day, while tending Jethro's flock, Moses found himself at the foot of Mount Horeb, also known as Sinai. A bush was shimmering with fire, though its leaves and branches were not consumed. Suddenly an otherworldly voice boomed:

GOD: *(VOICE IN THE BURNING BUSH)*
Moses, come no closer and remove your sandals—you stand on holy ground.

MOSES: Who are you?

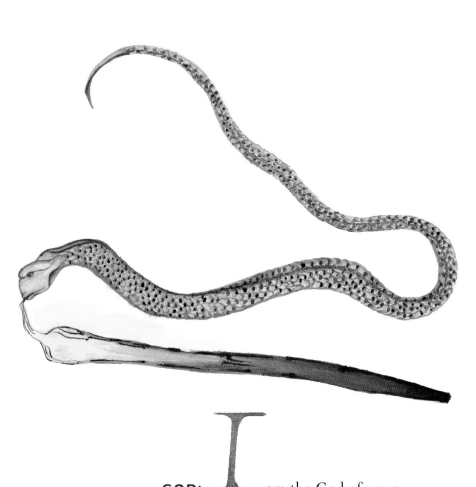

GOD: I am the God of your fathers—the God of Abraham, Isaac, and Jacob. As you've been living your simple shepherd's life, I've watched my people suffering in Egypt. Unable to bear their bitter bondage, they have been crying out to me. So you must go, Moses, down to Egypt—and bring them to this mountain. After this, you will lead them to Canaan—the large and lovely land I promised your ancestors.

MOSES: No one will believe I am your messenger. My tongue is slow and my speech is not eloquent. My words will rally no one!

GOD: Fear not, Moses. What is that in your hand?

MOSES: A shepherd's rod.

GOD: Cast it on the ground.

NARRATOR: Moses cast his rod down. I instantly it turned into a serpent. God then told him to grasp the serpent by the tail. At his touch, the snake turned back into a rod.

GOD: Now, Moses, slip your hand into your cloak and remove it.

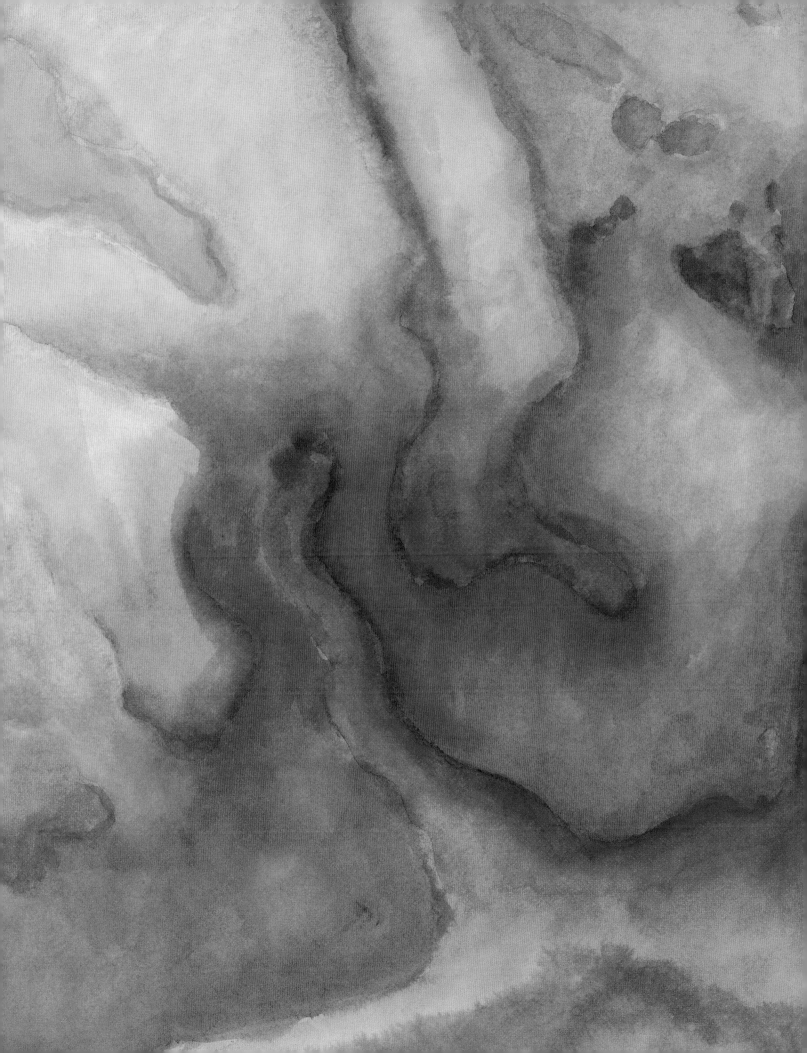

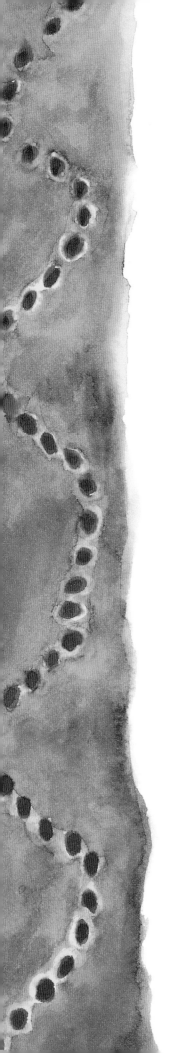

NARRATOR: Moses obeyed. When he withdrew his hand, he gasped. His healthy flesh was now white and flaky as snow. At God's command, Moses slipped his hand back into his bosom. When he removed it his scaly flesh had been restored to health.

GOD: If the people do not believe these signs and wonders, there will be others. And do not fear your slow speech. Your brother Aaron will serve as your spokesperson.

NARRATOR: So Moses and his family set off for Egypt. Halfway there, he met Aaron. When the two brothers reached Egypt, they arranged for a meeting with Pharaoh. Speaking on behalf of Moses, Aaron said:

AARON: Our God commands you to release his people so they can honor him with a three-day feast in the wilderness.

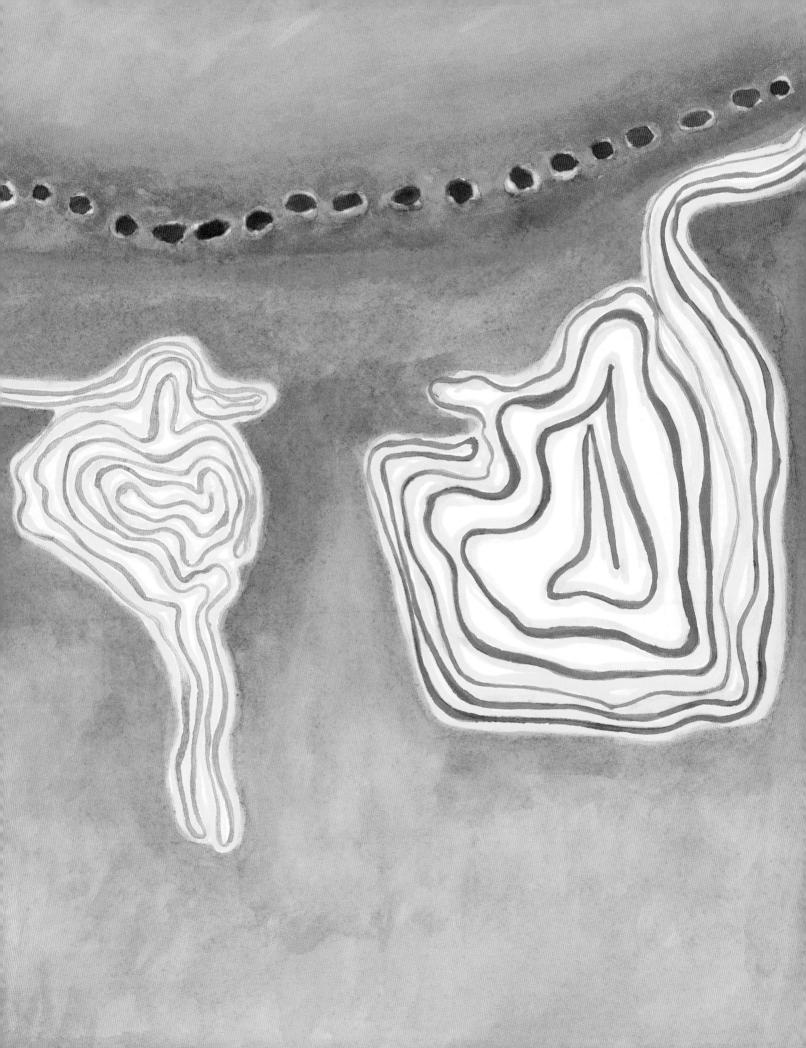

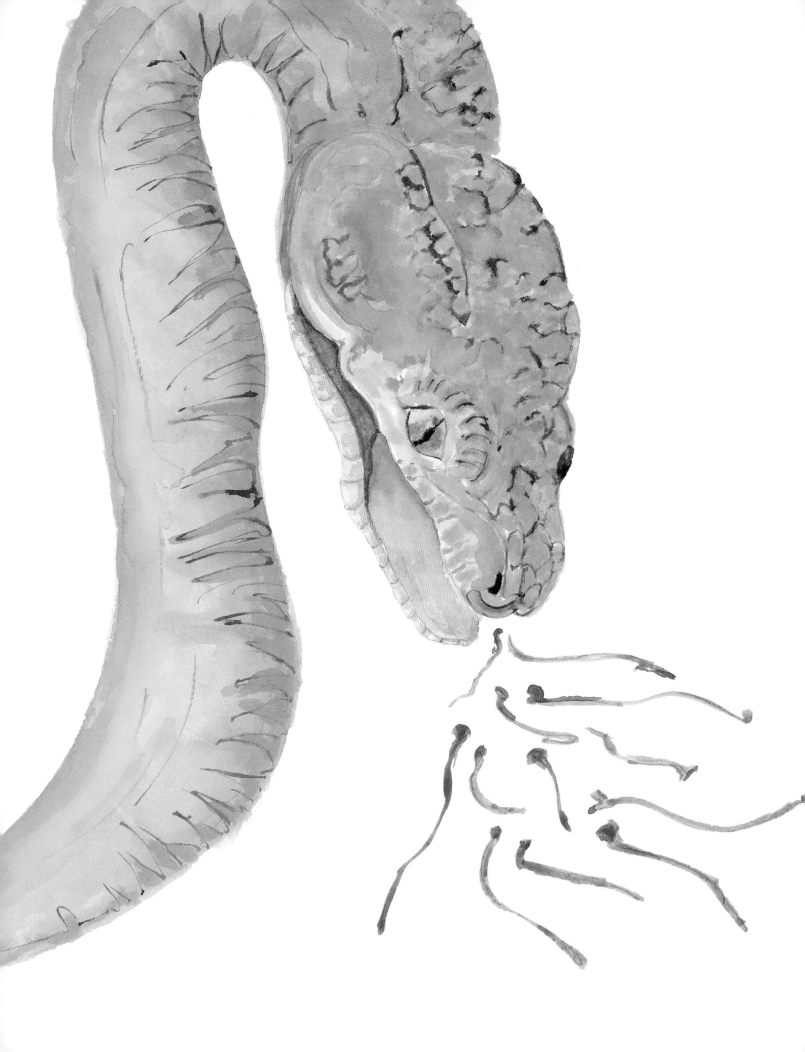

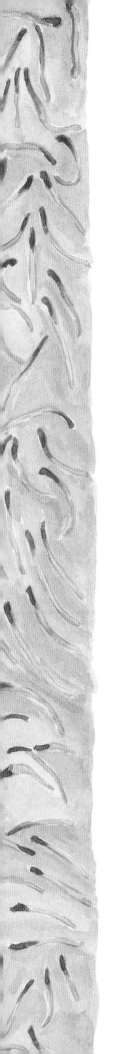

PHARAOH: Who is this god of yours? And why should I let *my* slaves worship him? They worship me alone! What can your god do that I cannot do myself?

NARRATOR: Moses threw down his rod and it turned into a serpent. But when Moses grasped the snake, it stiffened back into a rod.

PHARAOH: Nothing but a cheap trick. My magicians can do the same!

NARRATOR: Pharaoh summoned his magicians and commanded them to throw down their rods. They changed into small snakes. In the next moment, the larger snake of Moses swallowed the magicians' serpents.

NARRATOR: But Pharaoh was unimpressed and refused to let the Hebrews go. Instead, he increased their burdens, withholding the straw they needed to bind the bricks. God then instructed Aaron to stretch his shepherd's staff over the streams, the rivers, and the ponds of Egypt.

NARRATOR ONE: When Aaron did so, the waters turned to blood—even the water in the stone and wooden vessels turned to blood. Miraculously, the water in the slave province of Goshen remained pure. Still, Pharaoh refused to let the Hebrews go. God then said to Aaron:

GOD: Stretch your staff once more over Egypt's rivers, canals, and ponds!

NARRATOR: As Aaron did so, thousands of frogs leaped up and hopped through Egypt, entering the dwellings of royalty and commoners alike. They wiggled between the bedding, they sprang into the cooking pots, and they filled up the urns, temple bowls, and kneading troughs. The only place free of frogs was Goshen, home of the Hebrew slaves.

NARRATOR: When the Egyptian people became ill, Pharaoh had no choice but to summon Moses and Aaron back to his court.

PHARAOH: If your god removes these frogs, I will allow your people to make their three-day feast in the wilderness.

NARRATOR: So God caused the frogs to die. The Egyptians heaped them into enormous piles and set them ablaze. A terrible stench hovered over the land. But the moment the foul odor died away, Pharaoh withdrew his offer.

GOD: Moses, say to Aaron: Stretch out your rod and strike the dust of the land!

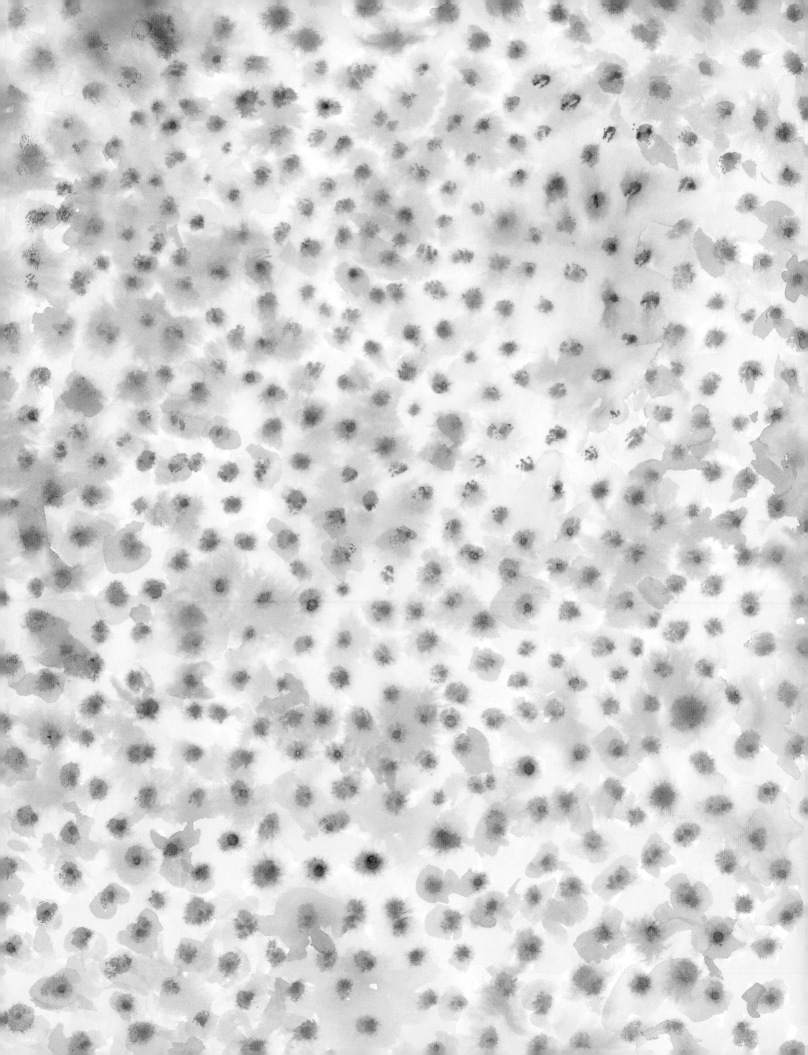

NARRATOR: Aaron did as commanded, and instantly the dust turned to lice. And the lice burrowed into the hair of humans and the fur of beasts. The Egyptian magicians attempted the same, but their powers were too weak. Afraid, the Egyptian magicians pleaded with Pharaoh to let the Hebrews go.

NARRATOR: When Pharaoh dismissed their pleas, God unleashed clouds of winged pestilence. And the buzzing clouds of gnats and midges and flies covered Egypt, causing the people to wail in misery. Only the Hebrews were spared. Pharaoh summoned Moses.

PHARAOH: Tell your god to remove this scourge! If he does, I will release his people.

NARRATOR: Again, Pharaoh reneged on his promise. And God had no choice but to send more plagues. First, wild beasts ravaged the land, and then disease killed all of Egypt's cattle.

NARRATOR: After that, boils bubbled up on the bodies of the Egyptians, and then hail the size of fists battered the fruit trees, breaking their boughs; only Goshen's trees were spared. And when the hail hit the ground, it burst into flame, and the fire ran in rivulets through the city streets—except for the streets of Goshen.

NARRATOR: Yet Pharaoh's heart remained stubborn; he refused to let the Hebrews go. So God blackened the sky with locusts. And the ravenous insects devoured every leaf and growing plant—other than those in Goshen. Facing mass starvation, Pharaoh summoned Moses and Aaron.

PHARAOH: If your god crushes these locusts, I will let your people go!

NARRATOR: Moses implored God to remove the locusts from Egypt. God obliged, sending a stiff wind that swept all the locusts into the sea. As before, Pharaoh failed to honor his promise.

NARRATOR: At God's command, Moses and Aaron stretched their hands to the heavens, causing a dense fog to roll across Egypt. The darkness was so thick it could be felt on the skin; the only gleam of light was in the slave quarters of Goshen. Terrified, Pharaoh called out to Moses and Aaron:

PHARAOH: Remove this suffocating darkness! If you do, you can take your people out of Egypt—though you must leave all your flocks and herds behind!

NARRATOR: But Moses refused to leave without the Hebrews' livestock.

PHARAOH: Then you and your accursed people will never leave! Now go away from me! I cannot bear the sight of your face!

NARRATOR: Moses returned to God, who revealed to him the awful details of the tenth and final plague.

GOD: In ten days' time, every firstborn male in Egypt will die at midnight. Not one will escape—neither the firstborn of Pharaoh nor the firstborn of the prisoner in the dungeon. And a loud cry will resound throughout Egypt— a cry that has never been heard or will ever be heard again.

But I will spare your children, Moses, and the children of your people. Tell the Israelites to slaughter an unblemished lamb. Then, with brushes of hyssop, instruct them to daub the lamb's blood on their doorposts and lintels. Seeing these markings, the Angel of Death will pass over them.

Ever afterward, this day shall be celebrated as a memorial. And this memorial shall be called Passover, and each generation shall tell the next how their ancestors were delivered from bondage in Egypt. And you shall keep it as a feast to the Lord.

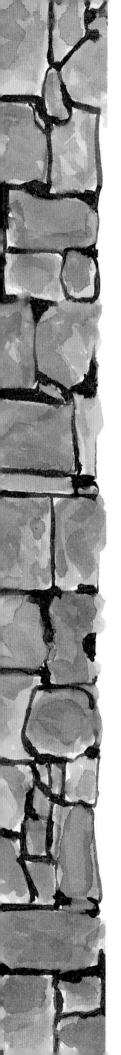

NARRATOR: Everything happened as God foretold. At midnight, the cries of mothers and fathers resounded throughout the towns and cities of Egypt. His own son destroyed, his will crushed, Pharaoh cried to Moses:

PHARAOH: Begone, Moses! And take your wretched people. And take the cattle and sheep you've so unjustly demanded! Go from here and never return!

NARRATOR: Fearful that Pharaoh would change his mind, the Israelites hastily prepared to leave, not even waiting for the bread in their kneading troughs to rise. And thus the Hebrews departed—six hundred thousand strong. And they journeyed far from the borders of Egypt, toward Canaan—the promised land of milk and honey. By day, they were guided by a whirling pillar of cloud; by night, a brilliant column of fire.

But Pharaoh's heart hardened again, as did the hearts of his courtiers.

EGYPTIAN COURTIER: Why have you done this? Why have you released our slaves?

EGYPTIAN COURTIER: How will we till our land?

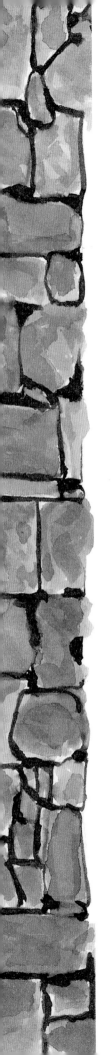

EGYPTIAN COURTIER: How will we feed our people?

EGYPTIAN COURTIER: We are ruined!

NARRATOR: Aware of the folly he'd committed, Pharaoh commanded his generals:

PHARAOH: Bring them back—every single one!

NARRATOR TWO: The Egyptian troops sped after the fleeing Hebrews. Soon the Israelites, camped on the shore of the sea, could hear the rumble of the approaching chariot wheels. They cried to Moses:

ISRAELITE: We are trapped! We will be killed!

ISRAELITE: Why have you taken us from Egypt just to die in the wilderness?

ISRAELITE: He is right! Better to have remained slaves in Egypt!

ISRAELITE: You have not led us to freedom—you've led us to death!

MOSES: Fear not. Stand still, and see what God shall do for you.

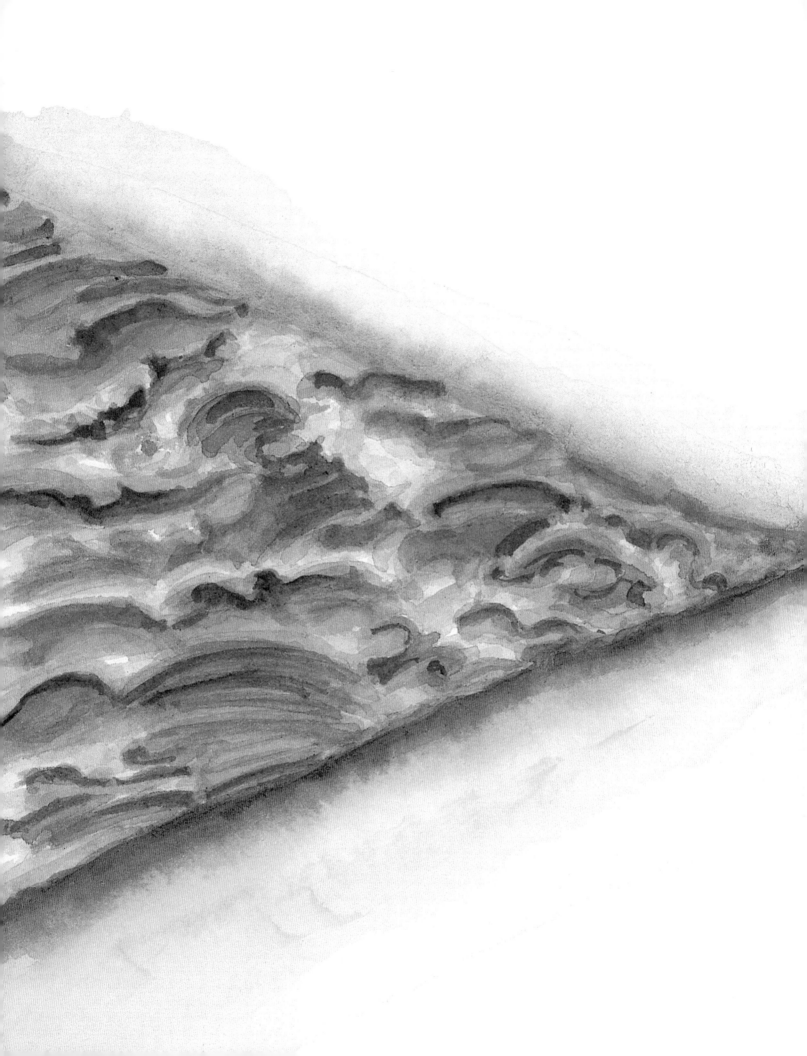

NARRATOR: Moses then stretched out his rod, causing an easterly wind to blow. With Egypt's militia bearing down fast, an Israelite named Nahshon broke from the crowd and boldly stepped into the sea. The wind stirred up the water, heaping it into two growing walls with a wide, dry path running in between. The Israelites followed Nahshon across the divided sea.

NARRATOR: The Egyptian army soon charged behind. But Moses did not panic. It was only when his people had reached the other side that he stretched his rod again, making the walls of water to roll back into place. For a few minutes, the Egyptian troops floundered in the waves. But quickly they were covered, and their cries were heard no more.

NARRATOR: Moses' sister Miriam rushed to the shore. As her tambourine jingled, she joyously sang:

MIRIAM: Who is like you, O God, among the gods? You triumphed gloriously; throwing horse and driver into the sea!

NARRATOR: And thus Israel was out of Egypt. And all day and night the Israelites celebrated, dancing and singing, oblivious to the dangers that lay ahead. *(break in storytelling)*

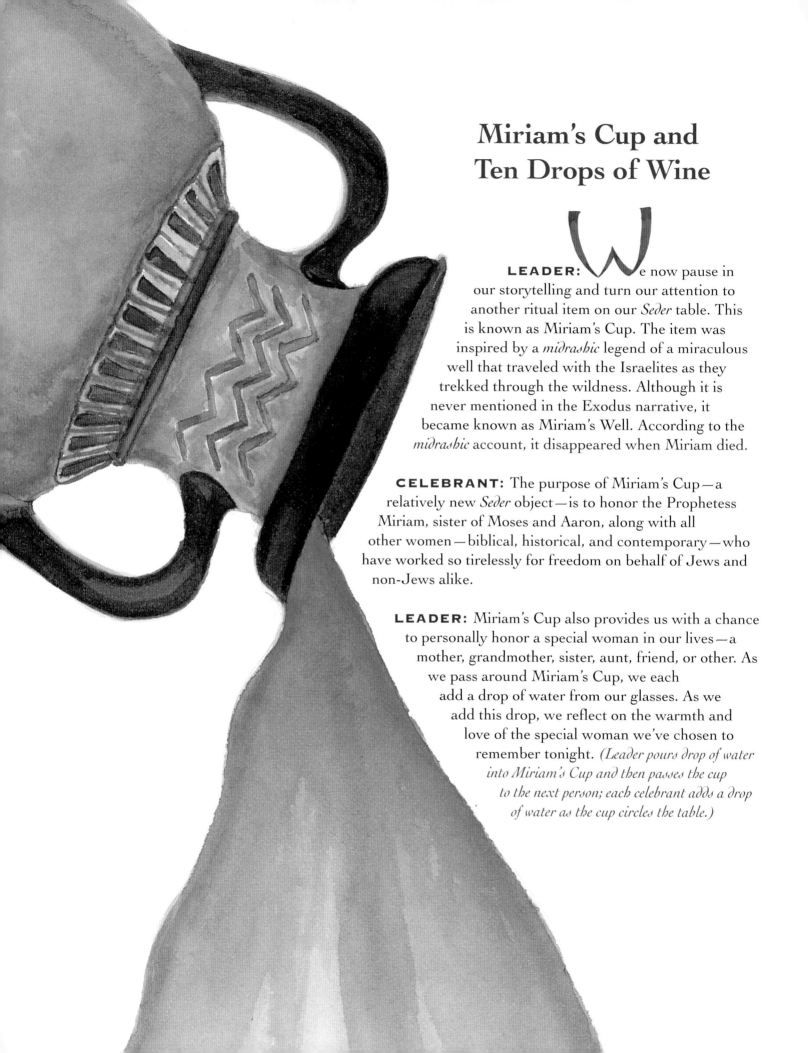

Miriam's Cup and Ten Drops of Wine

LEADER: We now pause in our storytelling and turn our attention to another ritual item on our *Seder* table. This is known as Miriam's Cup. The item was inspired by a *midrashic* legend of a miraculous well that traveled with the Israelites as they trekked through the wildness. Although it is never mentioned in the Exodus narrative, it became known as Miriam's Well. According to the *midrashic* account, it disappeared when Miriam died.

CELEBRANT: The purpose of Miriam's Cup—a relatively new *Seder* object—is to honor the Prophetess Miriam, sister of Moses and Aaron, along with all other women—biblical, historical, and contemporary—who have worked so tirelessly for freedom on behalf of Jews and non-Jews alike.

LEADER: Miriam's Cup also provides us with a chance to personally honor a special woman in our lives—a mother, grandmother, sister, aunt, friend, or other. As we pass around Miriam's Cup, we each add a drop of water from our glasses. As we add this drop, we reflect on the warmth and love of the special woman we've chosen to remember tonight. *(Leader pours drop of water into Miriam's Cup and then passes the cup to the next person; each celebrant adds a drop of water as the cup circles the table.)*

CELEBRANT: At this juncture in our *Seder*, we point out a *midrash* associated with the parting of the Sea of Reeds. The term "Sea of Reeds" is not a misnomer or alternative name for the Red Sea. It was a part of it, with shallow waters. While the Israelites could wade across it, the Egyptians, in their armor and their heavy chariots, drowned in it. Although the biblical account describes the Hebrews singing at the destruction of the Egyptians, the *midrash* tells another story.

CELEBRANT: In that version, the angels are cheering as the waters roll back into place, plunging the Egyptian to their deaths. But when God hears the angels' rejoicing, he grows angry and admonishes them: "Stop cheering, those are my people, too." Most of us don't believe in angels, but this story imaginatively makes an important point: while Jewish tradition sanctions the right to self-defense, it instructs us to always celebrate life, not death—even the death of our enemies. This lovely *midrash* teaches us that Judaism considers all people precious.

LEADER: This concept is expressed in the traditional Passover custom of casting drops of wine from our glasses onto our plates. With a finger, we each remove ten drops—one for each plague—and cast them onto our plates. This custom expresses our aversion to the punishment meted out to the Egyptians during our ancestors' deliverance. As long as others suffer—even our enemies— our own joy, symbolized by the wine in our glasses, is lessened.

CELEBRANT: As we perform this ritual, we reflect on the calamities plaguing our world today: the slaughter of innocents—both humans and beasts—as well as the pillaging and crowding of our planet, the plundering of our seas, the corrosive poverty, and the unjust wars. As we lessen our joy, let's silently commit ourselves to *kedoshim tehiya*—the striving after godliness and righteousness. Together, we now perform this ritual. *(Participants dip one finger into the wine remaining in their glasses, casting ten drops onto their plates.)*

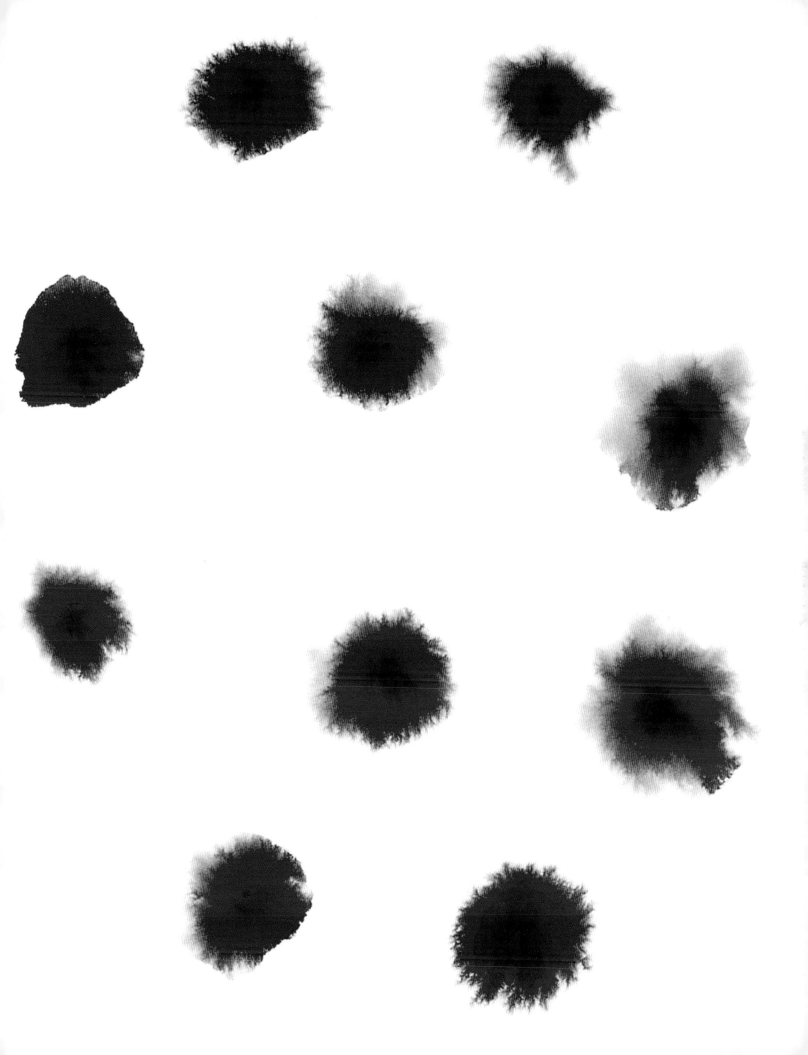

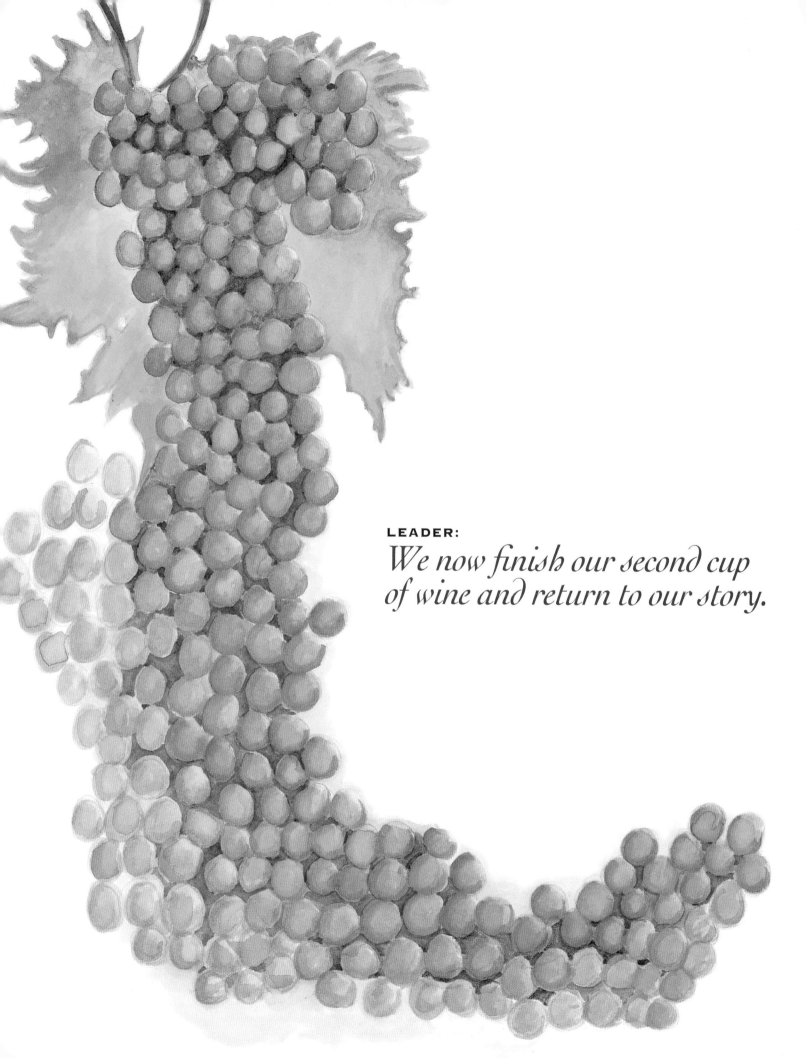

LEADER:

We now finish our second cup of wine and return to our story.

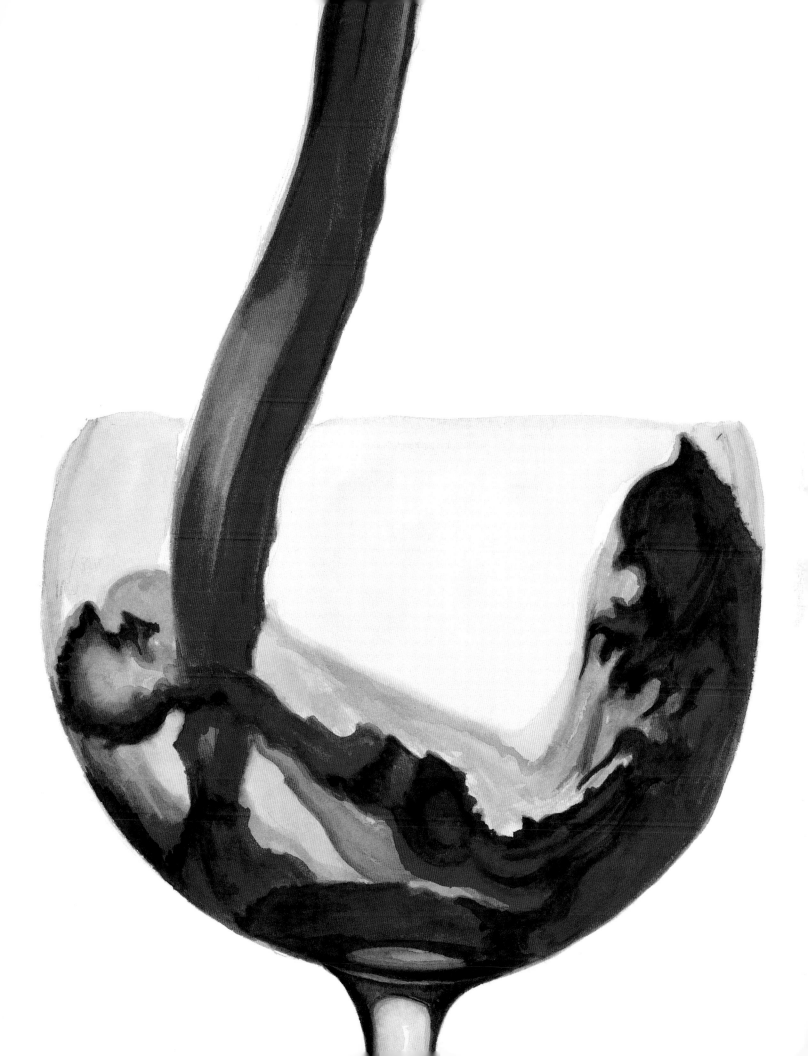

NARRATOR: Week after week, the Israelites journeyed south through the blistering heat of Shur. Finally, they reached an oasis called Marah. In huge throngs, they raced to its shining pools. But the water proved bitter and they spat it out.

ISRAELITE: What shall we drink?

ISRAELITE: We shall perish of thirst!

NARRATOR: Once again, Moses called out to God. And God told him to take the limb of a tree and cast it into the pool. Moses did so, and the waters of Marah turned pure and sweet. After satisfying their thirst, the Israelites journeyed on. As long as they had food, they remained calm. But once their stores ran out, their voices rose again in anger.

ISRAELITE: Moses! What are we supposed to eat? We will die of starvation!

ISRAELITE: He is right! Better we had stayed in Egypt!

ISRAELITE: We may have been slaves, but at least we had bread!

ISRAELITE: You've brought us from Egypt only to kill us with hunger!

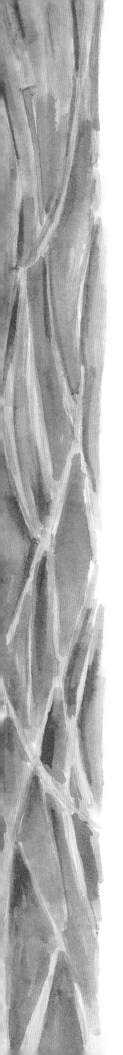

NARRATOR: With each passing day, the accusations grew stronger. Fearing the people might stone him to death, Moses called out to God. And God said:

GOD: Tell the people I will bring them meat and cause bread to rain down from the sky. And from this time forth, they will be able to gather their portion. But warn them not to gather in excess. And on the sixth day, they must gather a double portion—for the seventh day must be a day of rest.

NARRATOR: That very evening, a flock of quail flew into the camp. And the people set up nets and caught the birds easily. In the morning, the ground was dotted with sticky, wafer-like flakes that tasted like honey.

NARRATOR: The Israelites called this delicious foodstuff *manna*. And the pillar of cloud whirled on, leading them by day, and the pillar of fire burned brightly, guiding them by night.

NARRATOR: Finally, after forty-nine days of journeying through scorching heat and howling winds, thirst and hunger, the assembly reached the plains near Mount Sinai. Leaving his terrified people camped on the plains, Moses ascended to the smoking peak.

When he returned, he held two stone tablets inscribed with the spiritual imperatives known as the Ten Commandments.

(Storytelling ends.)

Counting of the Omer

LEADER: The receiving of these laws took place forty-nine days after the flight from slavery in Egypt. It is commemorated in a holiday called *Shavuot* or "Feast of Weeks."

CELEBRANT: Rooted in an ancient grain festival, *Shavuot* has been associated with the receiving of the Ten Commandments since biblical times.

CELEBRANT: Leading up to this holiday is a ritual called *Sefirat HaOmer*, translated as the Counting of the Sheaves or more commonly, the Counting of the Omer.

CELEBRANT: It is interesting to note that during the forty-nine days between these holidays, we count up rather than count down.

CELEBRANT: This unorthodox counting structure might reflect the idea that receiving the laws at Sinai is the apex of the Exodus story; without these ethical and moral imperatives the liberation from Egypt would have no meaning. It could also suggest that this is a time for "elevating" or improving our moral and spiritual selves; during these days, we can meditate on how to be more courageous, more disciplined, and above all, more loving human beings.

CELEBRANT: But whether or not we choose to formally mark the time between Passover and *Shavuot*, the Counting of the Omer connects liberty and the law, reminding us that without responsibility, freedom leads to chaos.

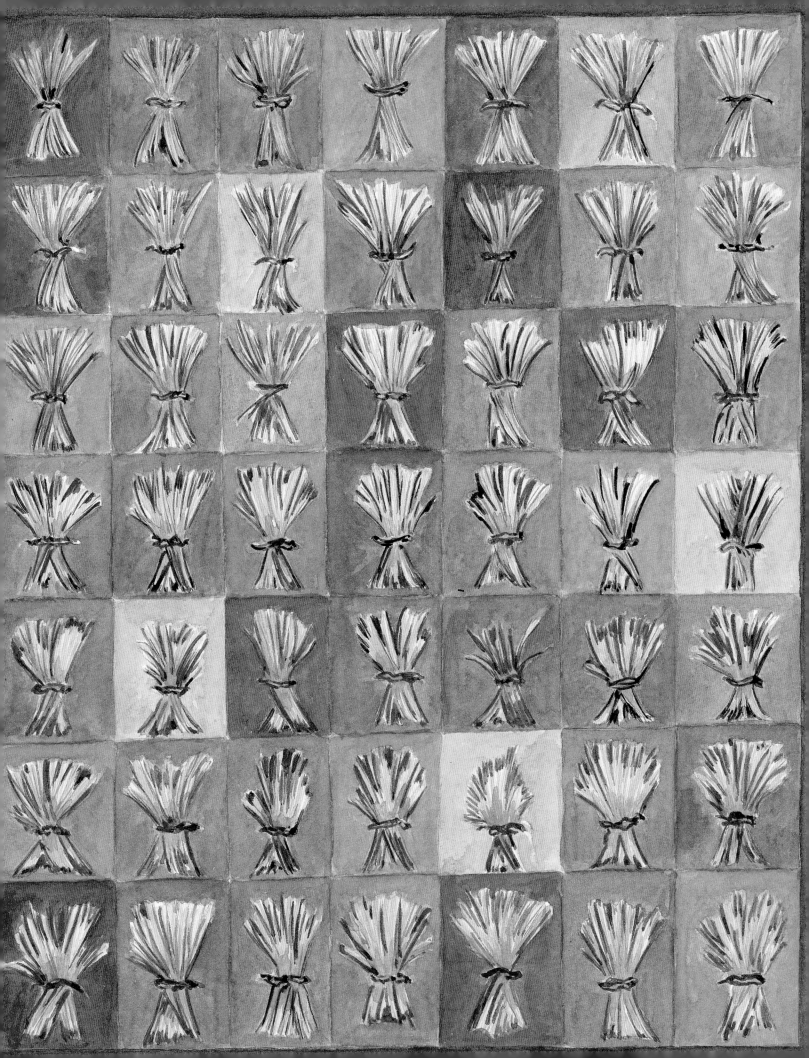

The Ten Commandments

1
You shall have no other gods before me. And you will love godliness with all your heart and mind.

2
You shall not commit idolatry.

3
You shall not take my name in vain.

4
You shall remember the Sabbath — the day of rest — and keep it holy.

5
You shall honor your father and your mother.

6

You shall
not kill.

7

You shall
not commit
adultery.

8

You shall
not steal.

9

You shall
not lie.

10

You shall
not covet
another's
possessions.

LEADER: The story continues with many dramatic episodes, including one in which the Israelites demand that Aaron build them a golden calf. After crossing the Sea of Reeds, the newly liberated slaves indulged in murder, thievery, and adultery. And although the scribes don't explain why Aaron allowed the people to build an idol, it is possible he thought that a tangible connection to Egypt might restore law and order. Or perhaps he was simply trying to appease the people until Moses returned from Mount Sinai.

CELEBRANT: Whatever the explanation, the biblical scribes inform us that Aaron told the people to melt down the golden earrings and bracelets of their wives and daughters. With this molten metal, he fashioned a bull calf for them to worship. At the sight of their adoration, Moses filled with anger and smashed the stone tablets against the ground.

LEADER: God was also furious and threatened to destroy the Israelites for breaking the orally spoken covenant against the making of graven images. Moses interceded on their behalf, and the people were spared. Afterwards, he fashioned a new set of stone tablets and inscribed them with the Ten Commandments.

CELEBRANT: Also known as the Ten Words or Sayings, these commandments not only informed the two other major monotheistic religions—Christianity and Islam—but also became the foundation stone of Western civilizations. Without this code of conduct, the world would be a very different and much less civilized place.

LEADER: The Ten Commandments fall into two categories: the first four detail the behavior between humans and the divine—which this *Haggadah* posits as a noninterventionist, unknowable force. The six commandments that follow describe the moral and ethical behavior between people. It is these human-to-human commandments that are absolutely essential to the creation and sustainment of personal, psychological, and political freedoms.

LEADER: The Hebrew words for "freedom"—
cherut—and for "engraved"—*charut*—are linguistically similar and
are linked in the tradition. This suggests that there can be no freedom
without moral and ethical laws—the kind of stark and universal
principles engraved in stone and revealed to the Israelites in the
burning wilderness of Sinai.

Tonight, we express our deepest gratitude to the visionary leadership
of Moses and the Hebrew scribes and sages whose world-altering
wisdom paved the way for the creation of enlightened societies
throughout the world.

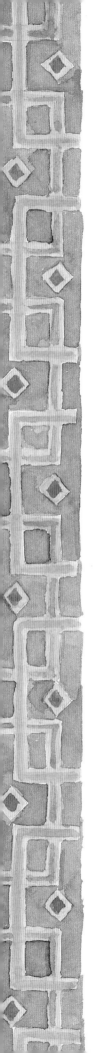

LEADER: We now pause in our reading, to share the Passover meal—a delicious meal that stands in stark contrast to the poor fare we once ate as slaves. At the meal's conclusion, the children will search for the hidden *afikomen*. Following its discovery and distribution, we will perform a few more *Seder* customs and then bring our ceremony to a close.
(Meal served.)

We now ask the children to hunt for the *afikomen*.
(Leader asks children to search for the afikomen; when it is found, the afikomen is broken into pieces—one for each celebrant—and they are distributed as a symbolic "dessert." The third cup of wine is drunk. The fourth and final cup of wine is then poured, but not drunk until the Seder's end.)

LEADER: It is customary to sing traditional Passover songs and chants after the meal. A favorite *Seder* chant is *Dayenu*, a Hebrew word meaning "it would have been enough." Although many versions of this chant exist, they all express a similar idea: we must acknowledge the blessings we have, even if they seem incomplete. The chant below centers on the theme of our search for a homeland. We survived two thousand years of dispersion. . . .

CELEBRANTS IN UNISON:
Da Da yenu! Da Da yenu!
Da Da yenu! Dayenu! Dayenu!

LEADER: and kept alive the hope of return. . . .

CELEBRANTS IN UNISON:
Da Da yenu! Da Da yenu!
Da Da yenu! Dayenu! Dayenu!

LEADER: We found leaders to make our dream a reality. . . .

CELEBRANTS IN UNISON:
Da Da yenu! Da Da yenu!
Da Da yenu! Dayenu! Dayenu!

LEADER: and won the United Nations vote to create a homeland. . . .

CELEBRANTS IN UNISON:
Da Da yenu! Da Da yenu!
Da Da yenu! Dayenu! Dayenu!

LEADER: We delivered Holocaust survivors to this new land. . . .

CELEBRANTS IN UNISON:
Da Da yenu! Da Da yenu!
Da Da yenu! Dayenu! Dayenu!

LEADER: and Arab, African, and Soviet Jews. . . .

CELEBRANTS IN UNISON:
Da Da yenu! Da Da yenu!
Da Da yenu! Dayenu! Dayenu!

LEADER: And if we deliver peace between ourselves, the Palestinians, and our Arab neighbors . . . that *will* be enough!

CELEBRANT: Another *Seder* favorite is *Chad Gadya*, which means "one little goat." Like everything in the *Haggadah*, there are multiple explanations for this song.

CELEBRANT: One suggests that the little goat—the *chad gadya*—is the Hebrew people, and all the other images represent the countries or forces that dominated Israel throughout her long history—beginning with the cat, representing the Assyrians, and ending with the Angel of Death, a symbol of the Nazis.

LEADER: Perhaps the simplest way to understand this song is this: no matter how difficult things become, in the end, human goodness—or godliness—always trumps the forces of oppression and destruction. Let's now sing the song.

Chad Gadya (Folk Song)

Chad gadya, Chad gadya
my father bought
for two zuzim
chad gadya, chad gadya
my father bought
for two zuzim.

Then came the cat
that ate the kid
my father bought
for two zuzim
chad gadya, chad gadya

Then came the dog and
bit the cat
that ate the kid
my father bought
for two zuzim
chad gadya, chad gadya

Then came the stick
and beat the dog
that bit the cat
that ate the kid

my father bought
for two zuzim
chad gadya, chad gadya

Then came the fire
that burned the stick
that beat the dog
that bit the cat
that ate the kid
my father bought
for two zuzim
chad gadya, chad gadya

Then came the water
that quenched the fire
that burned the stick
that beat the dog
that bit the cat
that ate the kid
my father bought
for two zuzim
chad gadya, chad gadya

Then came the ox
that drank the water
that quenched the fire

that burned the stick
that beat the dog
that bit the cat
that ate the kid
my father bought
for two zuzim
chad gadya, chad gadya

Then came the butcher
that slew the ox
that drank the water
that quenched the fire
that burned the stick
that beat the dog
that bit the cat
that ate the kid
my father bought
for two zuzim.
chad gadya, chad gadya

Then came the
Angel of Death
and killed the butcher
that slew the ox
that drank the water
that quenched the fire

that burned the stick
that beat the dog
that bit the cat
that ate the kid
my father bought
for two zuzim
chad gadya, chad gadya

Then came
human goodness
that destroyed the
Angel of Death
that killed the butcher
that slew the ox
that drank the water
that quenched the fire
that burned the sticks
that beat the dog
that bit the cat
that ate the kid
my father bought
for two zuzim
chad gadya, chad gadya

Conclusion

LEADER: Customarily, every *Seder* has closed with the words: "next year in Jerusalem." During the long and difficult years of the Jewish Diaspora, this cry represented our hope for a homeland—a place where our community, especially after the horrors of World War II, could finally feel safe. And yet, although we managed to establish the physical Jerusalem, the *spiritual* Jerusalem remains elusive. So tonight we raise again our fourth cup of wine and drink to the building of that golden city—the city of peace—in our hearts, in Israel, and throughout the world. Next year in Jerusalem.

(Celebrants raise and drink fourth cup of wine.)
This Passover, and in all the days following, we commit ourselves to supporting every idea, every effort, and every carefully crafted plan that seeks to lead Palestinians and Israelis, Jews and Arabs—indeed, all of the world's clashing people—out of the dark and narrow straits of fear and violence, out of the strictures of hatred and war, and into the spiritual Jerusalem—the *true* Promised Land—an open and peaceful place flowing with the milk and honey of justice, compassion, and freedom for all.

END

New York based but New Orleans born artist Jan Aronson has had more than sixty solo and group exhibitions. Her work is included in many museum, corporate, and private collections, both nationally and internationally.

Aronson is known for her nature inspired work that has over the years taken her to the Sinai, the Indian Himalayas, Patagonia, the Amazon, the American West and East, the beaches of Anguilla, and the Inca Trail to Machu Picchu. She often refers to these landscape pieces as "portraits of place" because there is more than just a lovely scene she wants to depict. Aronson is interested in probing the soul of a place, seeking to capture the mystery a place communicates to her. Each painting is a personal reaction and recording of what is special about the place.

In her portraits Aronson also tries to achieve more than just the likeness of her subject. She wants to dig beneath the surface of her subjects to reveal something of their inner workings, something about their psychology and what makes them special or unique.

Aronson received her MFA from Pratt Institute in 1973 and began teaching soon after. For the last twenty-three years she has concentrated solely on her studio work and has a working studio in Long Island City. She recently wrote a lecture on The Contemporary Portrait and presented it in venues in the US.

Aronson's work has been reviewed in numerous periodicals and newspapers since she began her exhibition career in the mid-seventies.

Illustrating *The Bronfman Haggadah* is the first such project she has undertaken and she is grateful to her husband Edgar for the opportunity to expand on her art vocabulary.

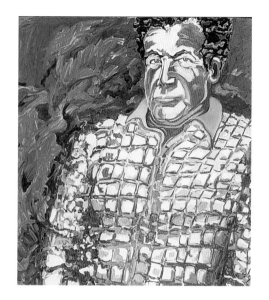

Edgar M. Bronfman is the grandson of Jewish immigrants from Russia who came to North America to seek a better life. Born in Montreal in 1929 and raised in a proudly Jewish home, Bronfman has always been active in Jewish causes, from the time of the founding of the State of Israel. He did not begin his own personal Jewish journey, however, until he was sixty years old and working on behalf of Russian Jewry in the former Soviet Union.

It was from that transformative experience that he began living a more consciously Jewish life, keeping Shabbat at home and engaging in Jewish text study. Bronfman's interest in the telling of the Exodus—particularly inspired by the story of Moses and his challenges in leading the Israelites from slavery to freedom—has been made manifest in the pages of this *Haggadah*.

Bronfman's love for the Jewish people informs his work at The Samuel Bronfman Foundation, which is dedicated to inspiring a vibrant and joyful Jewish future by working to build a knowledgeable, proud, and welcoming community. The foundation, named in memory of his father, is run jointly with Bronfman's son Adam. Edgar Bronfman's experience as the CEO of Seagram Company Ltd. for more than thirty years informed his work as the Founding Chairman of Hillel: The Foundation for Jewish Campus Life and his time as president of the World Jewish Congress, which he ran for more than twenty years.

In 1999, President Clinton recognized Bronfman's philanthropic efforts by awarding him the Presidential Medal of Freedom, the United States' highest civilian honor. Bronfman has also received the Chevalier de la Légion d'honneur from the government of France and the Justice Louis D. Brandeis Award of the 85th National Convention of the Zionist Organization of America. In addition, Bronfman holds honorary doctoral degrees from various institutions of higher learning, including Tel Aviv University, New York University, the Hebrew University of Jerusalem, McGill University, and Williams College.

This is his fifth book and first collaboration with his wife, the artist Jan Aronson. Bronfman has four sons, three daughters, and as of 2012, twenty-three grandchildren and two great-grandchildren. He hopes that they will use this book to continue telling the story of the Jewish people to their descendants and to claim their place in it.

2012 2013 2014 2015 2016 / 10 9 8 7 6 5 4 3 2 1

First published in the United States of America in 2012 by

Rizzoli International Publications, Inc.
300 Park Avenue South
New York, NY 10010
www.rizzoliusa.com

Library of Congress Control Number: 2012939189
ISBN-13: 978-0-8478-3968-1

Rizzoli Editors: Ellen Cohen and Robb Pearlman

Design by Doug Turshen with Steve Turner

Printed in China